Times Ten

Patricia Anderson

ISBN 978-1-0980-7442-5 (paperback)
ISBN 978-1-0980-7443-2 (digital)

Christian Faith Publishing, Inc.
832 Park Avenue
Meadville, PA 16335
www.christianfaithpublishing.com

Printed in the United States of America

Except the Lord build the house, they labor in vain that build it: except the Lord keep the city, the watchman waketh, but in vain.

—Psalm 127:1

X1

1987

The very first time I kissed a girl, I wanted to throw up. I didn't know whether it was because I was always taught that girls didn't kiss girls or because of the nauseating feeling that overwhelmed me when I realized I was actually doing what I had daydreamed about. Whatever the reason, I couldn't get to the bathroom quick enough before the dry heaves started. I could hear her voice in the bathroom area asking me if I was okay. In between the heaves, all I could say was "I'm good." I could see from beneath the door that she wasn't leaving, and the last thing I wanted to do was walk outside and see her face. I sat on the toilet, trying to regain my composure.

"I'm gonna need a minute," I whispered through the tears and the scratchy throat, hoping the entire time that she would just leave.

"Are you sure?" she asked.

"Yeah, you can go. I'm good. I just need a minute." I saw her feet step closer to the door, but just before reaching it, she paused and then turned around.

"I'll call you later," she said before the bathroom door closed with that annoying thump.

"Okay" was my response, but in my mind, I said, *Please don't bother*. I knew when she called that I wasn't going to answer.

I sat there a while longer, listening to the door open and close, toilet stalls opening and closing, flush after flush. I finally gathered enough nerves to get off the toilet and walk outside the stall. I went back to my dorm room. Then the reminder of what had just occurred in that very small space flew back into my mind, and my lips begin to quiver. I quickly grabbed my toothbrush and toothpaste and ran back to the bathroom and brushed my teeth like I had just eaten some bad bologna. That was probably the longest toothbrush my mouth had been subjected to. I wanted to remove all the tastes, all the memories of what had just transpired in my dorm room.

I looked at myself in the mirror. What about me made her even think it was okay to kiss me? I tried to replay in my mind all the events that had led up to me brushing my teeth at 10:00 p.m. on a Friday night with nowhere to go when the only time I ever brushed was every morning. (Yeah, they say twice a day and after meals, but who really does that, especially in college?)

I went back to my room and lay across my bed with nothing but questions and my emotions running wild. I wanted to cry. I wanted to scream. I wanted to call my mom.

No! Wrong answer. Oh my! What would my mother say? Oh no, can't tell her. I can't tell anybody.

What happened was wrong, and it was a mistake. I flipped around a thousand thoughts in my mind back and forward. The next thing I remember was someone knocking on my door, telling me I had a phone call on the hall payphone (this was well before the cell phone age). I knew who that had to be, so I yelled back, "Take a message!" Then I pulled the pillow over my mouth and cried.

The next few days, I was miserable. I hated myself. I hated her. I hated everybody around me. I didn't want to talk to anyone, and I didn't want anyone to talk to me. I finally decided to hang out with my girls (five of us usually hung out together). We were quite the wild and rowdy bunch. Tina—who was the no-holds-barred, cuss-you-out-in-a-minute, I'm-from-the-Bronx, you-better-get-out-my-face type—decided to ask me at the cafeteria breakfast table what my problem was. Actually, she didn't ask; she yelled at me.

"What's your f——n' problem! We ain't seen you in a few days, and now you sitting here, looking like you lost your best friend! You on your period?" All eyes, and laughter, were on me.

"Yeah" was the lie I told. Actually, I didn't tell it. I just agreed to what she said. It sounded good to me.

"Again?" asked Yvette. "You just had your period two weeks ago."

"Oh, well, must be stressing too much, and it came back," I said, peering at Yvette with that 'Let's just leave it at that' look.

That was Yvette. She knew everybody's business in the crew and kept everybody up to speed on one another. Of course, as much as we all were together, we all knew when others were on their period. That much was obvious. But the relief was in them believing it and moving on to something else, like what and where we were going for holiday break.

Since Tina stayed the farthest from Georgia and could only go home during the summer, we all took turns during the holiday breaks and spring break letting her stay with one of us. We didn't mind, and she loved it. She would always tell us that she had never seen so many trees in all her life. The only trees around the Bronx, according to her, were at the park. She probably felt like she was in a forest around here in south Georgia. The conversations went from holidays to classes and then to boyfriends. Unfortunately, I was the only that didn't have a boyfriend. I had a couple of guys that had tried to talk to me, but I wasn't really trusting anyone after my last breakup. It was rather funny how it all went down afterward, but in the middle of it, it hurt. And the hurt and embarrassment were still fresh.

Apparently, whoever came up with the dormitory concept thought it was a good idea to have the freshmen in one dorm, sophomores in another, and all the remaining upperclassmen in a separate building. For some of the guys, it was a player's paradise. They could have a girl in one dorm and one in the other. Freshman girls weren't allowed in the upperclassmen's dorm and vice versa. That was how I became a victim of Joel's web.

Joel fit the description of tall, dark, and handsome to the letter. He was well above my five feet seven inches in stature. He was in the Marine Reserve and was part of the ROTC program on campus, so he was well built with muscles in all the right places. When he smiled, he had this deep dimple in his right cheek that made me stare even longer at his attractive smile. We had been dating since the end of my freshman year. During the summer break, we talked almost every day. What separated us were the many miles and his obligation to the military for his summer program. I couldn't wait for the summer to be over so I could see his smiling face again and get lost in that dimple. Before returning to Savannah State, I signed up to be a Peer Counselor, which meant returning early for freshman orientation events that I would participate in as a counselor and also mentoring a group of freshman students. I was ecstatic to be back in Savannah more than anything because of Joel. He wouldn't be returning until another week with the rest of the returning upperclassmen.

The week was full of activities, and I became well acquainted with one of the other fellow counselors after a couple of days. She was a junior, and her name was Angela. After having a few conversations throughout the week, I learned she and Joel were from the same hometown. During one of the lunch breaks, I finally had a chance to talk with her.

"Oh, wow, you're from Donalsonville too?" I asked, knowing that as small as the town was, everybody knew everybody.

"Yes, I am. You know someone from Donalsonville?"

"Yes, I do," I replied, blushing from the inside from the mere thought of those dimples.

"Girl, who?" she asked.

"Joel Mathis," I responded, his name bubbling out of my lips.

"How do you know him?" she asked.

"He's my boyfriend," I said with emphasis, and as soon as I said it, she looked as if I had cut her in two.

"Really?" was all she said, and then she walked away.

I stood there confused about what just happened. Then one of my counselees came up to me with tears in her eyes, upset at the realization that she was away from all her family and friends. The conversation with Angela would have to wait. Someone needed a shoulder to lean on. I tried to catch up with Angela throughout the day, but the activities with the freshmen kept us busy. I had my group, and she had her own group. As the activities wounded down at the end of the week, the opportunity presented itself again, and I was able to have another conversation with Angela at the freshman mixer. I was more than curious about her response when I told her about Joel.

"Angela, you looked a little strange after I told you about Joel. Was there something that I said?"

She sighed and shook her head no. Then she paused as if she were choosing her words before she let them out of her mouth. "I really don't know how to say this, but I do know him—*very* well. I think that you are a pretty nice and good person, and I am not trying to cause any confusion, but Joel has a girlfriend. As a matter of a fact, he has a fiancée. She stays in the same building that I do."

The whole while she was talking, all I could see was her lips moving. The words were slowly beating against my ears and, at the same time, ripping my heart out of my chest.

No, no, no, no, no! was running through my mind. And then tears began running down my face. I didn't know whether to believe her or not, but there was something about the sad look on her face that told me it was true. Something coming from my insides was telling me, *You said it yourself. He was too good to be true.*

Angela said she avoided me intentionally the last few days because she didn't know whether she should tell me or not. She said she had seen it happen too many times and that it was one of those things that as a counselor, she had to warn the freshmen to be careful about. I guessed the counselor I had as a freshman didn't care because this was the first time I had ever heard about this. Since the freshmen girls were a separate dormitory, there were those upperclassman guys who would have a freshman girl they dated—or actually had sex with—and also had an upperclassman girlfriend as well because they didn't ever have to worry about the two meeting or interacting. They didn't have the same classes, they didn't reside in the same dormitory, and they would have never been seen with either one on campus. Since the freshman girls had a curfew, the guys would leave the visiting area of the freshman dorm and go visit the upperclassmen girls' living area, which didn't have a curfew.

The more she talked, the more I was breaking. In my mind, all the events of the past few months became a blur. I was drowning further in my tears.

Why didn't I see it? How could this have happened to me? How could he say he loved me? Why had I been such a fool? Why did I give my body over to someone who had someone else? What? Why me? When? How? I was crying beyond belief. Okay, wait a minute. Why are you crying? This isn't true. Maybe she's just mad and doesn't like him or me. That's it. None of this is true. Joel loves me, only me.

I began drying my tears and getting myself together. This girl was still talking and trying to explain. It was if she was trying to keep me from making a fool out of myself more than I already had done. I didn't want to hear anything else she had to say.

"Okay, I have heard enough," I whispered through the tears. "I don't want to hear anymore. I will wait until Joel returns, and I will get to the bottom of it."

"Yeah, okay" was her sarcastic response. "I am trying to save you any more heartache. But you go right ahead. When you need someone to talk to, you know where to find me."

"Yeah, thanks," I said, with no intentions of talking to her again. She had just put my world in a whirlwind with her lies and viciousness.

Joel would be back in a few days, and everything would be all right. Not only would he be back, but my crew would be back as well. The days and nights were endless, but the return of the girls was a welcome relief. I spoke only with Michelle about what Angela had said. I wouldn't dare tell Yvette; she talked too much. I couldn't tell Tina; she would really think I was dumb. And Lisa was really out of the question. Michelle couldn't believe it, and she wanted to go beat Angela up. I told her no. I would talk to Joel about it and go from there.

"Girl, please. Angela's big, fat, nasty self is just jealous 'cause nobody don't want her. Don't worry about it." Michelle laughed between the words.

"I'm not. Trust me." But something told me I wasn't too sure of that answer.

Two more days passed, and by Thursday, there was still no word from Joel. I was getting anxious, worried, upset, and scared, but most of all, I was lonely. After classes were done for the day, some of the girls wanted to hang out (Thursday was the beginning of the week-end for us). I decided to go to my room instead with hopes of seeing Joel. I didn't know where he would be staying since I hadn't heard from him in over week.

When I got back to the dorm, there was a message at the front for me. It was from Joel. He said he would be reporting to school the following week for late registration and that he would call me later. The disappointment and the agony grew worse. I went to my room depressed and was growing frustrated by the minute.

What if everything Angela said is true? What if I am being made a fool of? No! He said he loves me, me!

I fell asleep tired and depressed. I was awakened by knocks on my door. It was after 9:00 p.m. I opened it see Michelle looking like she was ready to fight.

She snatched me by my arm and said, "Girl, come on!" She pulled me out the room and down the hallway.

"Where are we going?" I wanted to know. I needed to know. If we were going to fight, then I needed to get my nerves up. Michelle was the bodyguard of the group. We could all hold our ground, but she was very hot-tempered. It felt like we were marching off to war. We marched out of the dormitory and headed toward the upperclass-men girls' dormitory.

"We can't go in there! We will get in trouble," I said, stopping at the entrance door.

"Stop being so scary, and come on!" She pulled me the inside the lobby, and as soon as we walked inside, Joel was there sitting and talking to some other girl, the same Joel that had left me a message that he would be returning next week, the same Joel that said he loved me. That same Joel with the eye-gazing dimple was now sitting there, smiling and holding hands with some other girl. His eyes met mine, and he froze midsmile.

Everything he ever said, every part of my body that he'd ever touched, every hair on my body began to tingle, and I wanted blood. The only thing I could do was turn and run. I ran back to my room with Michelle hot on my heels. I ran as fast as I could, and everything that was in my room that he had given me I began stuffing them in a bag—shoes, jewelry, stuffed animals, everything. The entire while I was stuffing, Michelle was talking and explaining.

"Girl, my homegirl works the desk at the dorm, and I went to go talk to her when I saw his black @##% through the door. So I ducked behind the counter so he wouldn't see me. Then when I saw him sit down with that other chick, I ran out and came and got you."

I was packing and crying and cussing and fussing. The nerve! The unmitigated gall this negro had to play me. Oh, I wasn't going out like that. I picked up the bag and told Michelle, "Let's go."

We walked back to the other dorm, and Joel was still sitting there as if nothing had just happened, as if he hadn't just seen me walk in there, as if my presence really didn't matter, like I was nothing.

I walked up to him and whoever she was and dropped the bag at his feet. "Here is all your stuff back, and don't ever worry about calling me again!"

His eyes grew as wide as I had ever seen, and he stood up and spat out viciously, "I don't know who you are or what you are talking about."

Then *she* stood up and asked him, "Joel, who is this?"

I didn't give him time to answer before I said to her, "Up until now, I was his girlfriend!" I wasn't mad at her at all. We both were victims, and he was going to get off easy. Her face twitched, and she looked at him as if he had some explaining to do.

He said to her, "Baby, don't believe anything this girl is saying. I don't know what she is talking about!"

"Oh, really?" I said, ready to fight. "So you don't know me or my phone number?"

"No!" he yelled at me with tears swelling in his eyes.

"Okay, so don't worry about calling 912-543-8989 again!" When I said that phone number, there was a look on *her* face like I had shot her.

Her lips began to quiver in the corners, and she looked him square in the face. "You used my calling card to call some other girl? You told me that was your cousin."

At that very moment, I felt her pain. I knew that he had lied to her as well, that she and I didn't know what we had gotten involved with—more so for her, because she was engaged to the liar. I felt some relief embarrassing him but was still hurting on the inside. I watched as she ran away from him and he chased after her. I couldn't believe this. I had been lied to. I had been used. I had been played.

Michelle looked at me and saw the hurt, the anger, the embarrassment on my face, and she tried to lighten the mood. "Girl, let's go fight him!"

I could only laugh, because I really wanted to do so. I wanted to cry, but I couldn't. I was too mad to be hurt and too hurt to be mad. We sat down in the chairs Joel and that girl had just vacated. Michelle's homegirl wasn't going to kick us out or report us. Most of the folks had already gone to some party somewhere or out in the city. We sat there not saying anything, just looking at the wall, unsure of what had just happened and why. I didn't want to be in there any longer. Sitting there, hurting in silence, wasn't going to change the events.

"Let's go," I said.

We went outside and headed toward the parking lot, taking the long route back toward the dorm. I saw Joel and that other girl walking toward us. He was walking slightly ahead of her, and the closer he got, the uglier he became. He walked up to me, and I could see he had been crying. His eyes were red, and there was still snot in his left nostril. I wanted to punch him in balls and call him a liar, but before I could, he hissed at me.

"You didn't have to do that! You were wrong for that! Tell her you just made it all up," he demanded.

He can't be serious! He wants me to lie to her to save him from her wrath?

"I wish I would! Boy, bye!" I could see him clench his teeth and put both his hands in his pockets, like he was putting them there to keep from hitting me. I took a step back just in case he felt brave enough to do so.

Michelle turned to walk away. She grabbed my arm and said, "Let's go. This #$@% done lost his mind."

Still facing him, I saw him pull his hands back out of his pockets. His right hand wasn't empty. I saw the small handgun, and at that very moment, I was no longer hurt or disappointed. I was pissed.

"Really? That's what you wanna do?" I asked, and I snatched my arm away from Michelle and stepped back toward him. "Go ahead then. Shoot! Shoot me! SHOOT! You real bad. You pull a gun on a female! SHOOT!" His lips started quivering, like he was scared as well.

I stepped even closer and said it again, "Shoot!"

Before he could even raise the gun to shoot, *she* grabbed his hand with tears in her eyes and told him to put the gun away. Then *she* told him, "Let's go, baby. She ain't worth it. It's okay. We're going to be okay." He looked at her face and put the gun away.

I stood there, and the only thing that I could say was "Dumb, both of you." I waited until they walked away hand in hand back across the campus. I wasn't about to turn my back on him or her. Yeah, they were meant for each other. He was scary, and she was dumb. He got caught cheating and pulled a gun on me. Where did they make these Negroes at?

That was the horrible end to my so-called relationship. Sitting here at the table with the girls and listening to their discussion about their relationships brought the wave back over me, but I soon dismissed it because he certainly wasn't worth any more of my thoughts. Someone else was trying to invade my brain, and I knew that wasn't the route I wanted to go. That unspoken kiss in my dorm room between me and Faye could never be spoken of again. I didn't have to worry too much about seeing her around campus because she didn't live on campus. The only time I would run into her would be at band practice. She was a saxophone player (woodwind section), and I was a trumpet player (brass section), so I didn't have to be too concerned about sitting next to her or even rehearsing in sections with her. I would make sure after practice was over to avoid her like the plague. That was the plan.

The first day at practice, all went as planned. I could only breathe a sigh of relief. The next day of practice went the same.

"Okay," I said to myself, "I can do this."

The following day, Faye wasn't at practice. "Okay, that's even better."

However, the day afterward, during my classes, I found myself wondering where she was. A couple of times, I had to slap myself for even thinking about her. My mind went back to the forbidden kiss, and what I began to remember wasn't all that bad.

Have you lost your mind? Yes, you are losing your mind. At one point, it would be an enjoyable thought, and the next time, it would be repulsive and nauseating. *This can't be happening,* I thought. I guessed that as long as I was avoiding her, I felt in control. But to not see her made me realize that I really wasn't in control as I had thought. I was confused.

I had been raised in the church. Every time the doors opened, we were there. It wasn't an option or up for discussion. The only person who didn't get carted off to every church service, choir anniversary, one hundred women in white, Men's Day program, Easter program, Christmas program, Mother's Day program, revival meeting, youth program, or any other event someone had was my daddy. He was the only one that wasn't always there. As for me and my eight brothers and sisters, we were always told "You better get your butt ready, 'cause you going to church!" So I knew it was wrong. I had been away from my parents' house and my mother's stern grip for only over a year, and I was having all this trouble—a scary, crybaby boy pulling a gun on me and a brave, bold girl kissing me. I was becoming more and more confused.

The following day, Faye was at band practice. I got butterflies in my stomach. *Well, smarty, what's the plan now? Just ignore her. Yeah, that's a good plan.* I put my mind on the music and let the blare of the brass drown out my thoughts. By the end of practice, I was exhausted from all the heat, the sand fleas, and the band director's need for perfection. I was drained and had to sit down before I trudged back across campus with the heavy horn and case. I threw a towel over my head to get some shade.

Before I could close my eyes good, I felt a cool breeze brush past me and felt the heat of another body sit beside me. I heard the breathing and low whisper.

"I am sorry about the other day in your room. I thought I had gotten a few signals from you, and I took it too far. It won't happen again. I hope we can still be cool," she said and then waited for a response.

I mulled around *Go to hell!* in my head, but I didn't want to start a fight. I had had enough of violence to last me for a while. The only thing I could say was "I'm straight. You good. Just keep your distance." I snatched the towel off my head and grabbed my case and stood up and walked off. I didn't care what she said or did. I wasn't sitting there with her any longer.

I made it back to my room and felt the urge to throw up again. I hated myself. I hated her. I hated my thoughts. I hated Joel. I didn't want to be at his school or around these folks. I plopped down on the bed and looked across the room at my roommate's bed. I felt a chuckle come from nowhere. I had kissed a girl! There wasn't a really big difference other than the fact that it was a girl. Her lips were softer. Her hands were gentle and smooth. Her eyes weren't as harsh; they were soft and sad looking. She really wasn't all that cute. She said I gave her some vibes. I looked at myself in the mirror. I wasn't ugly. I had long beautiful hair, a small frame, slightly bow legs (my daddy's folks). I had guys trying to talk to me all the time. I ignored them while I was in a relationship. What made her think it was okay? I replayed the events from that day in my mind.

We had left band practice and was headed toward campus. She wasn't one of my girls, but since she was in the band with me, we had hung out quite a few times after band practice. None of my girls were in the band. They said it was too hot for all that. She said she had a couple of hours to kill before she had to be home and asked if she could hang out. I said sure, and we went back to the dorm and sat around listening to some music and talking about the folks in the band and some of everything else. She was a native of Savannah, so she knew lot about the area and had plenty of lies to tell. One of her stories sounded just like that—a big *fat lie*! Before she could finish, I told her to hush and threw my pillow at her to cover up the lie she was telling. She threw the pillow back and hit me pretty hard. The next thing I knew, I was up and went to swinging. She grabbed my arm before I could hit her, and we started wrestling. She was a lot stronger than I thought. She did a quick twist move, and we ended up on the bed, me on the bottom. She had my arms pinned, and I couldn't move them. Both of us were breathing heavily. I told her to get off me.

"Move! You're squishing me!" I growled.

"Nope, not until you apologize," she said.

"Apologize? Apologize for what?" I asked, out of breath.

"For trying to hit me."

"Girl, move! You hit me too hard with that pillow!"

"Well, I apologize, I'm sorry. Now you apologize."

She wasn't moving off me. I wasn't about to apologize. I remember turning my head away from her face and feeling weird but comfortable. For a minute, I didn't want her to move. I wanted her there. I turned my head back and looked at her, trying to give her that "Get off me or else" look. Our eyes locked, and her face drew closer to mine. She began kissing me, and I didn't make her stop. When she began grinding on me, she loosened her grip, and I was able to get my arms free and push her off me. I couldn't get out of that room fast enough.

Now that I'd had time to replay it, I guessed I did give her a vibe. There must have been something in my eyes when I looked in her face that said, "It's okay. You can kiss me." Ugh, I need to wear sunglasses. That wasn't okay. Initially, yes, it felt good and soft, but when I remembered who it was I was kissing and who I was, the thought was overbearing. I was just as guilty as she was. I had extended the invitation beyond retrieval. Well, I wasn't going any further with her or that. I quickly came to my senses and got out of that room and those thoughts. I went to the lobby, and there were a few folks sitting around, playing spades. I sat to the side and said I got next.

"Who's your partner?" was the voice that came up from behind me. It was Troy.

"I don't have one. You can be my partner," I said.

"Can you play?" he asked.

"I can, a little," I replied.

"Oh, well, I can't be your partner. I need someone who can play 'cause I like to win."

"I will be your partner, Lane." It was Michelle, who popped up in the middle of the conversation. "Ignore that boy. He's about to carry a whooping back 'cross campus."

Everybody started laughing and telling the other players to hurry up so they could see the end results of the trash talking. The entire while the other game was going, Troy and Michelle were going back and forward with the noise, and I just laughed. It felt good to laugh.

It was finally our turn to play. One of the winners let Troy have her spot so it was Troy and the recent winner against me and Michelle.

"So what we playing for?" Troy asked.

"We playing for a win!" I said, and Michelle and I slapped a high-five across the table.

"Nah, we need to make this interesting. Let's put some money on it," Troy said as he shuffled the cards.

"Boy, please, we in college. We broke!" Michelle told Troy like he was her child.

"Well, I will take whatever y'all got!" he said.

"Nothing!" Michelle and I said at the same time.

We all laughed, and Troy started dealing. He said, "We'll see."

Troy was the biggest jokester around. He was one of the star football players and was also the dorm clown. He was cute, but we all knew he had a girlfriend that would cut your throat for looking at him too hard. The game went back and forth in score and trash talking. On the last hand, we lost. We couldn't leave that table fast enough and get away from the embarrassment of having talked all that trash and still lost. Troy was rubbing it in and still smiling and laughing and talking cash money.

"Boy, go home!" Michelle told him. I decided I had had enough for one day and told everybody bye.

"Where you going?" I heard Troy ask.

"Away from you!" I said and shot him a bird. He was cool and all, but he had worked my nerves.

Classes the next day went well, and I wasn't dreading band practice anymore. I believed she got the message. There wasn't anything left for us to talk about. I wasn't interested. I got back to the dorm and went and put my stuff in the room and remembered I needed to go to the store. I left campus for a while and came back and called my sister. The hall payphone we had to use was at the beginning of the hallway. As soon as you came downstairs, the payphone was in the corner to the left of the stairwell. I heard someone come down the stairs, and then I felt my keys being pulled out of my back pocket. I had a bad habit of putting them in my back pocket. I turned around, and it was the dorm clown walking down the hall with my keys, telling me I wasn't getting them back. I talked to my sister a few more minutes, not concerned about Troy and his foolishness. I finished my phone call and went to my room door. I open the door and stood in the hallway and told Troy to get out of my room and stop playing around. He came to the door to leave, but instead he pulled me inside and put his hand over my mouth.

At first, I thought he was just being his usual "dorm clown" self until he said, "I came to get what's mine." And he threw me on the bed.

I started screaming. "No! No! Stop!" at the top of my voice. He wasn't listening. I started crying and still screaming, "Stop! Stop!"

He was licking and kissing me all over while pinning me down and was trying to get my pants off.

I heard a door slam down the hallway, and I started yelling louder. "Help! Help!"

I heard someone walking down the hall, dragging their feet in their bedroom shoes. Somehow I got free, and when I did, I ran to the door and out and ran down the hall, and there was Margaret, headed to the bathroom to take a shower.

"Help me! Get him out of there!" I was shaking.

"Who?" She stepped toward my door, and the room was pitch-dark. She didn't go past the face of the door, and she turned around and said, "Who? I don't see anybody."

"Troy!" I said, still shaking.

"I don't see him in there. I can smell his cologne though." He wore the loudest, sweet-smelling cologne, and everybody knew him for it.

"You didn't hear me screaming?" I asked.

"Yeah, but I thought y'all were in there wrestling and fighting again, like y'all always do." She had a point. Me and the girls liked to practice our wrestling and fighting skills.

She walked toward the door again and looked inside. "There is no one in there," she said before she went on her way down the hall.

I stood staring into the room and couldn't see him, but then when I stepped back in the hallway, I saw an eyeball between the crack of the door that was partially open.

"Get out!" I said.

He came from behind the door, and I stepped far enough that he couldn't grab me. He walked out of the room, shaking his finger at me and laughing. He went down the other end of the hallway away from the exit. I grabbed my keys and went to the phone and called my sister. I told her what had just happened. She was in the city, but she got me in touch with my uncle who was on the police force. I called him, and he said since I was on campus, it was a campus security matter and I would need to contact them and then we would go from there.

The hours following that was a blur. There I was again, somebody's fool. How could someone I know and trust attack me? I had said no! That fight to get out that room with Troy brought other memories to the surface—the hurt and shame of a time all the way back to when I was a little girl and my dad's best friend would come into the room at night and suck on my chest. I didn't even have breasts. He would take his hand and play between my legs and put his mouth down there.

He would always tell me the same thing: "Shhh…don't say anything. You don't want no trouble."

I felt dirty and disgusted. I felt like nobody cared what was happening to me. I felt like a toilet that any and everybody used when they felt like it. I didn't want that from Troy or anybody unless I chose to do so. It seemed like lately no one was giving me a choice.

The next couple of weeks could not have been more dramatic. Since Troy was Mr. Popular, my pressing charges was like I had put the bulls-eye on my back. I got plenty of stares and cutthroat looks from folks. The word got back to me that he said I was lying and that I had wanted to give him some. He was another dumb boy. I wasn't at all thinking about that or him. I felt like I was being drawn in another direction. I was very uncomfortable being in that dorm room and among those girls that had his back, and I requested a transfer to another room. The only room that was available was one in the freshman dormitory, and I was allowed to move over there, considering everything that had happened. The good thing was, I didn't have a roommate anymore. I was in a room by myself. I didn't have to be in the room with someone who didn't like to bathe or wash their sheets.

We eventually went to court, and after my testimony, his testimony, and with Margaret as the only potential witness, he was found guilty. I was relieved at the outcome, but on campus, I became the outcast. I went to class and to my room. Football season was long over, so there was no band practice. Michelle would come by and check on me, but I was pretty much a loner. I cried many nights and wanted this to be over. I refused to go back home. There was nothing there for me. I was born and raised in the country. Picking peas, pulling weeds, chasing hogs, grinding cane were not what I wanted to do for the rest of my life.

I had lived a sheltered life. We didn't have cable. Telephone usage was limited. I wasn't allowed to have a boyfriend until I was sixteen, and I dated him up until my senior year. Then one day, his sister came to school and told me that he had another girlfriend where he was stationed in the army. How crushing was that? AWFUL. He was the only guy I fell in love with before I left for my mom's house for college. Now look what I had been through. They didn't put all this in that manual they gave us at freshman orientation. Who was supposed to prepare this naive, country nerd from the class of 1986 for all this?

I decided that I had to go. I wouldn't go home, but I would transfer to another college. My brother would be at the college up the road in Statesboro, and I decided to go there as well. I needed a new start. I needed to be where I didn't know anyone and no one knew me. I could put Faye, Joel, Troy, and all this drama behind me.

Yes, that's it! I felt a wave of relief come over me, like I was being released from punishment.

I told Michelle on her next visit what my plan was. She didn't look too thrilled.

"You leaving? For what? You gonna just run off and leave me?" Her response was just a little weird. She of all people knew everything I had been through—almost everything (she didn't know about Faye). She did know how much I hated being there. The crew had dispersed pretty much. They were all doing their own thing, falling in love and not hanging out anymore. I had my own share of problems and didn't want to be around folks anyway.

"I gotta get away from here. This place is depressing, and I can't go through another two years like the last two. I need to go!"

"Well, I understand, but I'm gonna miss you. You my girl!" she said with a sad face.

"Yeah, and you mine."

With those words, she started crying. I held my arms out to give her a "group hug," but she pushed my arms away.

"I don't want no hug. I wanna fight you."

We both started laughing. I could always count on her to make the heaviest situation light.

The next few weeks, I started working on my application and getting myself prepared to transfer. I also started seeing a lot more visits from Michelle. She would hang out in my room with me, and a couple of times, she would spend the night in the other bed across the room. We would talk until we fell asleep, and I felt even more relieved. She was like the sister I never had. I had three sisters—two older and one a lot younger. My older sisters always said I was too young and that they didn't have time for me at all. My youngest sister was a baby when I left home, so I really didn't have someone to talk to about my deepest secrets, thoughts, or problems. I had my best friend in high school. We used to talk all the time, but I had graduated a year ahead of her. I could tell her anything, but she wasn't here, and phone calls weren't free. I hoped she wasn't having all these problems her first year of college.

The excitement of leaving this place outweighed the stares, the looks, the drama, and the boredom of being isolated. I got news of my acceptance, and that was the icing on the cake. The end of spring quarter couldn't come fast enough. Michelle asked me one night what I was doing for the summer. I really hadn't thought about it. I needed to work somewhere. I told her that I knew for sure. Her eyes grew wide with excitement.

"Hey, you can come stay with me and my folks for the summer. I will be working at my dad's store, and I am sure you can find a job in Atlanta."

"You sure it will be okay?" I asked, uncertain if I could handle driving around Atlanta. I had my own car, but that was a big step. I knew the only work back home for me would have been work in the fields, so I agreed as long as it was okay with her parents.

"Girl, they don't care, as long as you don't have fleas!"

I couldn't help but fall out laughing.

X2

The drive to Atlanta wasn't that bad. I was looking forward to something different and moving past the drama and the foolishness. Michelle was a good friend and welcomed relief. We arrived at her home, and her parents welcomed me as if I were one of the family. I spent the first week learning my way around DeKalb County and filling out applications. I finally got a part-time job at a distribution center and then, shortly after that, a full-time job at a fast-food restaurant. I worked and the more I worked the farther my mind drifted away from all the drama of my first two years of college. Days seemed to be filled with work and sleep.

The part-time job at the distribution center only lasted a couple of weeks, which left me with a little more free time. Michelle's folks reminded me of my own family, except theirs was a lot smaller. She only had one brother compared to me having my five brothers and three sisters. She was the perfect definition of *spoiled*. She was funny, though, and would have me rolling in tears at times as she talked about her family and some of the kids she grew up with. Out of my years in college, she was only thing that had been persistent and dependable. She had been working at her father's store since we had gotten back, and we both finally had a weekend free after about month of grueling schedules. She informed me that we had been invited to a talent show with her boyfriend and he would bring one of his friends to accompany me. I was rather leery at first, but I didn't want to be a party pooper. And I didn't have to be by myself, so I went ahead. The show was exciting and very entertaining. There were some talented people in Atlanta! Much more I can say for my company. He was a straight bump in the road. I feigned stomach cramps as soon as the show was over so I could go back to the house. Michelle got the hint, and we left. As soon as we hit the car, I exploded in laughter.

"Girl, what the hell was that?" I wanted her to explain.

"I don't know. At least he had nice shoes!" she shot back, still laughing.

"I can't believe you did that to me!" I was still laughing.

"I didn't do it to you. His face did!" She snapped back before doubling over with laughter.

"You coulda told your boyfriend no! Emphatically *no*!" I told her.

"I didn't know that was who he was talking about, and he ain't my boyfriend." She was laughing at the beginning of that sentence, but by the end, she was drop-dead serious. "He's a boy, and he's my friend, but he ain't my boyfriend."

Okay, now I was confused, because this was my first time hearing this. I had heard her talk about Tim all the time, and she had said we were going out with her...friend. Oh, she never did say anything about boyfriend. She just said *friend*. I had assumed.

I felt a little tension in the air, so I decided to cut the elephant into small pieces. "Well, whatever he is, at least he was cute and better-looking than the road kill I was sitting with."

She cut her eyes at me and couldn't hold out any longer before she was laughing and beating her hands on the steering wheel. "You're right, but you are so wrong. Road kill don't wear nice shoes," she said.

We laughed and joked until we made it back to her house. It was late, and I was tired. I fell across the bed and had to know the reason for the undertone earlier. She sat at the foot of the bed, kicked off her shoes, looked at her feet, and did not say anything. I felt the air thickening with tension, so I cut at it again.

"So why did you get so snappy when I said Tim was your boyfriend?" I asked, but she didn't respond or look my way.

So I nudged her arm, and she moved away and stood up. Then she turned around and looked at me. Her eyes were watering as if she wanted to cry but didn't want me to see it. I felt the air leaving the room by the gallons. She just stood there staring at me, and I recognized that look. It was the same look Faye had before she kissed me. My mind started racing, and my heart was beating faster than a drumroll. The only difference was that this time, it wasn't fear. I wasn't afraid. I enjoyed her jokes, her laughter, her dependability, her readiness to fight in my defense, and her sensitivity, and she was actually rather cute. Something had changed since Faye. I wasn't repulsed at the thought. My mind and my body were welcoming the thought and the possibility. I guessed we had a deeper connection than I realized. I wasn't going to jump to conclusions. It could just be me imagining or having other desires. Maybe the interaction with Faye previously had stirred up something that had been hidden deep within the fiber of my body.

After what seemed like the long drive to New York, Michelle's mouth began to move, but no words were coming out. I tried to focus on what she was saying, but I was too lost in her lips. Before I could even ask what she had said, her lips were pressed against mine, and I felt the softness, the warmth. The butterflies that were in my stomach went farther south and created a warm gush. I didn't resist. I didn't push her away. I didn't get nauseous. I didn't feel the urge to go and brush my teeth. I found a feeling that was different from any other kiss, and I enjoyed it. All the years of my mom dragging me to church and everything that I had been told became a distant memory. None of that mattered at that moment. The only thing that mattered was how I was feeling and how good it felt. The kiss became more than a kiss, more than a hug, more than a cuddle, more than what I realized was possible. There were more parts of the body to explore, and we explored them all. I remember falling asleep happy, satisfied, and loved.

The next morning was awkward. Nothing was said. We avoided eye contact, and I felt the overwhelming urge to want to run away. That totally contradicted last night. I was confused once again. The silence wasn't helping at all.

I wasn't going to allow the silence to create even more confusion, so I asked, "What happened?"

The look on Michelle's face didn't match what came out of her mouth. "Who you asking? You asking me like you weren't there," she shot back.

She was right. Dumb question. "I mean I know *what* happened. I just want to know what brought all that on," I said still, unsure of my words.

"Obviously, you weren't listening to anything I said last night," she stated emphatically.

She was right. I hadn't heard a word she had said. I was too fascinated by her lips and the way they looked when she formed her words. So I owned up to it.

"No, I didn't. I was looking at your lips too hard to listen," I said matter-of-factly.

That broke the thick cloud in the room, and she smiled a brief smile before letting out a deep sigh. "I was trying to tell your big head that I love you and it wasn't the way a friend was supposed to love a friend. I mean, I have been around girls who date girls, but I never have even thought about it or tried it, but there was something different about you. I felt comfortable with you, and I wanted more than just to be your friend. I remember actually being jealous a couple of times when you would spend more time with some other crew, and I was like, I must be losing my mind. I just know I didn't want to see you with anybody else," she confessed.

I was listening to everything that she said, and at the same time, I was questioning myself. Was there a sign on my forehead that said I kissed girls? Was there a scent that was coming out of my armpits that said I liked girls? What was it? My sister used to tease me all the time and say, "You like girls. You funny." Was there something I was not seeing? It was not something that I imagined or dreamed of. I knew that my experience with guys wasn't something I could say was 100 percent great. If I put all my experiences in a category with the opposite sex, they would come out on the piss-poor side. I had been molested as a child on numerous occasions by different ones. The two guys that I fell in love with in high school broke my heart and dumped me for someone else. The college guys weren't too much brighter and smarter either. I was attacked by one. I was lied to, cheated on, and then threatened with a gun by another. Trusting them wasn't high on the list. The friendship I shared with Michelle was refreshing. It was safe, it was genuine, it was loving, and it was comfortable. She just happened to be the same sex. Yes, that was it! Everything was making sense in a crazy sort of way. All the desirables were there; it just so happened to be desires for a female.

Michelle had stopped talking, and she was looking at me as if I needed to respond. I hoped I wouldn't say something retarded because I didn't know how much of what she did say I actually heard. Now was not the time to be a clown. I cleared my throat and sat up in the bed. I needed her to understand me, and I needed to understand me.

"I don't know what to say. I know that I care very deeply for you. This is all new to me as it is new to you. I can't say that I understand all this or I know how all this is supposed to go. I just know that I enjoy you and I enjoyed what happened last night. I don't know if will even happen again, but I do know this is all foreign territory for me and I am a little scared. I can't make any promises nor can I say that I am 100 percent sure this is something I want. I think we should just see how it goes and go from there, if that makes any sense." The more I said, the more relieved I felt. I could tell that she felt the same way because her mood lightened.

"I won't tell—if you won't tell!" she said, laughing with a small amount of fear. I understood what that meant, and I felt the same way. This was not something I was going to write home to my mother about. As far as we were concerned, we were our own little secret.

The days and nights after that were a whirlwind. I felt like we were double agents. During the day and in front of her parents, we were just the best of friends. At night and behind that closed door, we were more than friends. We were lovers, mating, enjoying each other's bodies. This secret life made the days and weeks fly by faster than we wanted. Before we knew it, the summer was over, and it was time to go our separate ways. I couldn't go back to where she was going. That school had too many bad memories, and I would never be able to fully enjoy my days there, considering everything that had happened.

We had come to the point where we had to have another serious conversation. What would we do, and how would the double life be affected? We decided to just continue on as we had been and to see each other when we could. The only stipulation was that we couldn't get in a relationship with anyone else, male or female, without discussing it with each other. We agreed, and we spent the last night together just talking. I was going to miss her. I was going once again going to a strange place with no friends. I would be starting all over again. This time, I would get it all right. Maybe somewhere in the both of our minds, we knew we wouldn't last, but just the thought and the conversation gave us hope.

X3

————— ✦✦✦✦✦ —————

Fall 1988

This college was totally different from the one I had just left. The campus was enormous. The dorm rooms were bigger and newer. There were stores, restaurants, and places for activities on campus. The one thing that was missing was the friendly people. It was an entirely different atmosphere. Going from a historically black college to a predominantly white university was like the biggest shock. I joined the marching band, and that opened up the bubble I was in. I was around people who was just as crazy as I was majority of the time. It was classes during the day, on the field practicing in the evenings, and the weekends were football frenzy.

Michelle and I talked on the phone when we could catch each other in the dorm, but that wasn't very often, with me having classes, practice, and football games, not to mention the after parties and the before parties. I wasn't a drinker like the folks I was hanging out with at times. I had tried a cooler once, and it was horrible. It tasted like rotten fruit mixed with a little spoiled milk. Just hanging out and dancing and watching everyone else was fun.

About two months into the school year, Michelle said she wanted to come up for a visit for a weekend. I checked our football schedule and gave her a weekend that the football team would be playing an away game that the band wouldn't be going along. I wasn't really looking forward to her visit because I had a roommate. I didn't want to get caught in any awkward positions or deeds with our secret nightlife. My thoughts and presumptions got the best of me, and I began to dread her coming. It was as if she would be bringing a part of me that I was trying to leave behind. Yeah, as long as we talked on the phone, laughed at each other's jokes, said how much we missed each other and that we loved each other over the phone, that was okay, and I was good with that. For some reason, we had returned to the friends that we had started out being, and that was a good place. Her coming might stir up that monster that was lurking in the shadows. I wasn't dating anyone, wasn't talking to anyone, and wasn't interested in anybody. I was enjoying the freedom of being by myself. The weekend finally came, and our first sight of each other was a little awkward. It was though the time we had spent apart had smothered that fire and that burning sensation that we had when we were behind closed doors.

The hug that we gave each other told the rest of the story. The fire was gone. We were back to where we were before we crossed the line. It was in that moment that I realized that we were both two lonely and heartbroken people who reached out and found each other but realized that it wouldn't work or continue as it had been. We were only an hour apart in distance, but emotionally there was a Grand Canyon between us. I drove us to a park that was a short distance from campus so we could just talk. I wanted to know what it was that wasn't being said, and I had to be sure that I wasn't jumping to conclusions. I didn't want to be the first to say anything. That was the safest route. I knew how I felt, and I didn't want to hurt her feelings. She began talking, and this time, I wasn't distracted by her lips. I actually heard the words that were coming from her mouth.

"I have had a lot of time to really think about all this since we have been a part," she began, not looking at me at all. "I enjoyed being with you and all the things that we did. I know that I love you and everything, but I can't go back to the stuff that we were doing. It's not right. I can't tell anybody, and then when folks start talking about other girls who are like that, I feel embarrassed. I sometimes wish I had never kissed you and just kept it all to myself."

The more she talked, I felt a wave of relief coming over me, and at the same time, my heart was slowly aching. I couldn't bring myself to say anything because I didn't know if I was supposed to agree or fight her about what she was saying. Was this girl breaking up with me?

She kept talking. "I didn't want to talk to you over the phone because I had to come and see for myself if it was real or not. When I saw you in the parking lot and I hugged you, I felt nothing. I wanted to fight you for making me feel like this and then not being there to help me through it. So I said I was gonna come up here and tell you that we can be friends if you still want to but we can't be anything else. No more of that nasty stuff."

For some reason, the way she said *nasty* made me know she had come to her senses and wasn't going to be changing her mind. Now this was where it got really weird because all this time, I felt the same way but for her to actually say it made it hurt just a little.

I wanted to say "Good" but decided instead to not be so nonchalant. I told her, "If that's what you want, then I am fine with that. Just remember, this was your decision."

"I know, and I'm good with it," she shot back.

There really wasn't too much else we had to say after that. We sat and watched a few people play in the park until the silence had said enough.

"Well, I am going to head back to where I belong," she said as she stood up.

I stood up as well and held out my arms for a hug. The look she gave me told me she was just as torn as I was. She hesitated, but we hugged anyway. We both knew this was the last time and probably the last of the frequent conversations. We would need time to get beyond the attachment and attraction we had felt. We were letting go and moving on. When she left, I felt that emptiness again. I felt alone in a dorm and campus full of folks. I felt as though I didn't fit in and that there would never be anyone to fill that emptiness. I was lost to my own thoughts. The only thing that kept me occupied was the constant repetition of classes, band practice, parties, football games.

That was interrupted by the end of football season. I had met one young lady in the band, and we began to hang out. This time, it was just a friend, and I would make sure of that. I wanted to get something right this time. That other part of me was over now that Michelle had severed the cords.

We did all the things friends were supposed to do. We went shopping. She did my hair, something I didn't know how to do. We talked, but it wasn't a constant requirement. Tosha was different. She was a genuine girl—nail polish, hairdos, makeup, and frilly shirts. I wasn't allowed to wear nail polish and makeup in my mother's house, so I grew to dislike it. I didn't get my feelings hurt if I had asked her to wear it like the other girls were doing. The first time Tosha put makeup on my face and I looked in the mirror, I almost didn't recognize my own self. I remember wearing makeup once, and that was for the high school pageant that I was in. Tosha tried her best to make me feel comfortable with it on, but I couldn't get the hang of it. I wore it a couple of times after that, but it was too much work.

Tosha came over to my dorm (she stayed in the dorm across campus) excited about and bubbling about signing up for a sorority.

"Girl, I have you a set of papers as well. Let's do this!" She couldn't contain herself.

"Are you sure?" I asked.

"Yes, why not? It will be fun!" she said.

I didn't know what world she came from, but I had already heard the stories and had already seen at the last college this wonderful world of pledge life and sorority life that she was so thrilled about. Since she was truly a friend, I wasn't going to let her down, and this journey we would take together.

We submitted our paperwork and had to go for the first round of interviews. Tosha told me everything I needed to know. Her mother and her sisters were both already in the sorority. She didn't realize that I was only the second person in my family to go college and that no one had even mentioned a sorority to me until she did. I felt relieved when one of the interviewees was one of my hometown girls. She had graduated the year ahead of me, but we were in the band together and had some of the same advanced classes and electives together. She asked me why hadn't I pledged at the previous college before I transferred. I told her that I was undecided and had a few unfortunate incidents and got distracted. The interview went well, and we were all told that we would get a notification if we would proceed any further. Tosha got a call back, and I didn't. When I inquired as to why, I was saddened and hurt that my past had once again interfered with my present. Apparently, they had gone and questioned some of their other sorority sisters at my previous college, and they told them that I ran with a crew of girls that were trouble-makers. Only part of that was true. We were a crew, but we weren't troublemakers. We just didn't let folks run over us. There had been an incident where a pack of sorority sisters showed up at Tina's door right across the hall from me, wanting to know why she had spray-painted her car. Tina being Tina cursed them out and told them not to come knocking on her door with no BS about some paint. They assumed just because she had a sign on her door with the same color of paint that she was the culprit. The louder they got, the more the hall doors started opening and looking. The only ones that stepped in to back Tina up was the crew.

When they saw us standing there with her, they backed off but not before Tina yelled at the leader of the pack, "You might want to ask your boyfriend who spray-painted your car. It could have been his other girlfriend!" That was the worst insult, but they only came for what they thought was going to be a weak individual. The leader wanted to lunge, but her judgment got the better of her. We were surrounding them on all sides, and they changed their mind really quickly. From that one incident, I was labeled as a troublemaker and blackballed for the rest of my college life.

Nevertheless, I was somewhat relieved. I didn't want to be both-ered by all those prissy, high-class, nose-in-the-air females anyway. I was only trying to support my friend in what she wanted to do. What did this poor, country girl know about a sorority? Nothing. And I didn't want to know. I left with a bucket full of mixed emotions and feelings. I knew that when Tosha made it, that would bring a great divide for us as friends. Then I would be back to where I was—alone in my own skin on a campus full of strangers.

The following week went by really slow. While I was walking back to my dorm one day, I walked past a girl on the way home that had a T-shirt on that said "Raw Deal." She stuck a flyer in my hand,

and I kept walking. Her shirt was right. *Raw deal* was what I had been getting. I looked at the flyer, and it was advertising the intramural basketball games for the week. I was once again at the misery of my own self, so I decided to check out a few games later in the week just to keep myself busy.

I had high hopes that the game would be interesting to say the least. I played basketball in high school. Well, let me rephrase that—I was on the junior varsity team a year or so. I provided moral support for the team until the love of music led me to the band. Plus, my mother said she had spent money on a trumpet when I was in elementary school, and she wanted her monies worth out of it. So the bulk of my high school was spent in the band. I still had the love for the game, though, and this reminded me of all those times I sat and watched all the excitement from the bench. This time, I didn't have on a uniform. I saw the girl that had shoved the flyer in my hand. The game started, and she had the same position I had—a bench warmer. Well, that made me feel a little better. There weren't that many people in the gym, so any seat would put me by myself. The game started, and the point guard for Raw Deal got the ball and took the first shot. Swooosh! A three-pointer!

Okay, this may be interesting, I thought.

The rest of the game followed the first shot. Raw Deal was the real deal and smashed the other team. The next game started, but it wasn't quite as wonderful, so I slid off the bleachers and headed back toward the dorm. I decided to drop by and see if Tosha was in and if she had made any progress since we had last talked. I made it to her dorm and knocked on her door, but she never answered. I was leaving when I saw the point guard for Raw Deal coming through the lobby.

"Hey, great game! I enjoyed it," I said, and I must have caught her off guard. She looked around as if I was talking to someone else.

"Who, me?" she asked before she flashed the biggest smile. "Well, gee, thanks. Come out again same time next week. We will be at it again," she said as she walked off. I didn't answer, but I knew I would be there. All the way back to my dorm, that smile was glued in my mind like a bright light had been turned on in my dark brain. It was magnetic, and just like that, I was drawn back to the next game.

The game was pretty much a repeat of the last one. The crowd was just as thin as before, and Magnetic Smile was in control the whole game. As far as I was concerned, she was the only player on the court. The sign on my forehead must have been on because after the game, she came and plopped down beside me and started talking like she already knew me.

"Did you see that?" she asked me.

"What?" I pretended I didn't know what she was talking about.

"How awesome I was!" she said and flashed that smile that was beginning to draw me to a place of uncertainty.

"Nope, I didn't notice. Kinda boring if you ask me." I tried to hold back a smile, but the wounded look on her face broke my heart. I caved in. "Yeah, you were pretty good." I had to admit it. She was a pretty good player.

"By the way, I'm Tonie, and I am glad you came out," she said as if she knew I was there to just watch her.

"Oh well, it's something to do other than class in the middle of the week," I replied.

"You are so right, Pam," she said.

"I know, and my name is Lane, not Pam." As soon as it came out my mouth, I realized that it was a setup because that magnetic smile went from ear to ear. I could only hang my head in embarrassment at my simpleness.

"What are you doing later?" she asked and kept talking before I could answer. "A few of us from the team are hanging out, and you are more than welcome to come."

"I don't know," I said. "I don't have anything planned but sleep. Plus, I don't really know y'all that well."

"It's on campus, and this will be the perfect time to get to know us," she said.

"I guess it will beat being bored," I responded.

"Yes!" she said as if she had scored a three-pointer. I had to admit, but not to her, that I was ready to go wherever she was going. "I need to go get out this uniform, and I can meet you in front of my dorm in about forty-five minutes," she said as she stood up to leave.

"Okay, I will just watch some more of this game. Maybe I will see another 'awesome player,'" I said, smiling as the sentence ended. The look on her face told me she didn't take that as a joke.

"On second thought, you can come and wait in the lobby while I shower and get changed," she shot back.

For some reason, I thought that was cute, that she didn't want me to watch anyone else play but her. So I got up and walked back to dorm with her, and she was talking the entire while, telling me her lifelong story in less than ten minutes. By the time we made it to the dorm, I realized I enjoyed her more when she was just smiling. She told me shouldn't be long, and she was right. I wondered if the water even made it to her feet before she jumped out of the shower.

I didn't know why I thought that her appearance off the court would be different from her appearance on the court. I had only seen her in the team shirt and matching shorts. She returned looking about the same, with an over large T-shirt and a pair of basketball shorts. If it weren't for her large breasts, she would pass for a boy. Okay, now I wanted to change my mind, and she must have noticed.

"What? You don't like my outfit?" she asked.

"Not at all. But I don't have to wear it," I responded.

"Well, everyone can't wear tight Levi's like you," she said and snapped her fingers twice in the air.

I couldn't help but laugh, and that night and the next few weeks, we were inseparable. During one of our many conversations, she asked me if I wouldn't mind taking her home to visit her mom one weekend. She said while we were there, we could hang out with a few of her friends back home. I told her as long as she was buying gas, we could go wherever she wanted. That was the deal I made with everyone that asked for a ride since all the people that I had been around didn't have a vehicle, except Michelle. My car moved on gas, not promises or magnetic smiles.

The weekend came, and we were on our way. Her mom stayed in Savannah, and that place didn't have any great memories for me, but I took a deep breath and decided not to share that horror story. We arrived at her mom's, and I was expecting the same mother-daughter relationship that my mom and I shared. She walked in the apartment, introduced me, and the next question she asked her mother was what she had in her house to drink.

"You know where it is," her mother said as she waved her hand and walked off.

Tonie went the refrigerator and pulled out a beer and asked if I wanted one. I frowned, shook my head no, and was not feeling too welcomed. Tonie could sense my irritation and told me not to worry. We wouldn't be in the house too long; we were going out. We would be meeting up with her cousin and a few of her friends later. She told me to make sure that I had my driver's license in case we were carded.

"Are we going to a club?" I asked.

"Yeah, and you will enjoy it. Trust me," she said, sounding so sure of herself and me.

I was more than curious and began to realize this trip wasn't to see her mother but to hang out at a club. I was beginning to see more of the real Tonie, and she was slick. We got dressed, and for the first time, she put on something besides an overlarge T-shirt and basketball shorts. She called her cousin, and she told her we would meet them all at the club.

We met outside the club, and with exception of height and a different haircut, Tonie and her cousin looked like twins. She introduced herself and the rest of the girls with her. I immediately noticed a pattern. There was a girl who could have easily pass for a boy paired up with a "girly girl" like me. Standing in the line to get in the club, I saw more of the same, along with a few guys who reminded me of the guy in high school that used to get picked on for being so feminine. He would walk down the hall, and the guys would part the hallways like the Red Sea when he walked past them or even turn and go the other way. This time, no one was running; no one was making fun of anybody. We were all herding into the club. I inched a little closer to Tonie, and she grabbed my hand and told me "Don't worry" again and again.

The thump of the music could be heard from the outside. Its pulsating beat was unlike anything I had heard before. I had never been to a club that I could remember, and I knew I had definitely never been to a gay club. This was a first, and I could feel myself been drawn to that music and that song "Back to Life." This was a version

I hadn't heard before. This was a little faster with another song mixed in it. I was a little scared, but that music seemed to be calming my nerves, and I began to have the same beat and pulsating feeling going through my hands and legs. I felt like I was beginning to float into another place, and when we got inside, it was just that. They didn't even check our ID. We paid and went on in, and all my fears were left outside. I had stepped into another world, one filled with flashing lights, vein-pulsating music, and more folks that looked like me. The people that I only had previously seen one or two of here and there were now surrounding me like a crowded shopping mall. There were three floors of wall-to-wall gyrating guys who looked like girls and girls who look liked guys and then those who looked like me—lost and trying to decide where to fit in.

Tonie excused herself and came back with two drinks and offered me one. I shook my head and frowned my nose at the same time because she wouldn't have heard me say "I don't drink" above the pumping of the music.

She sat her drink on the table and yelled in my ear. "Just try it! You will like it, and it will relax your nerves," she said.

I didn't ask how she got it, knowing we both were under the legal age. I only took a sip, and at first, it was syrupy sweet, but when it went down my throat, it burned a little almost like NyQuil. I took another sip, and it wasn't as bad as the first one. But I couldn't stand the taste, so I sat it down and refused to drink anymore. Tonie shrugged her shoulders and, after downing her drink, picked up mine and proceeded to do the same.

Okay, she's a drinker, not impressed.

After a couple of songs, I could feel a little warm and felt the urge to move with the music. I began to dance where I was standing, and the more I danced, the freer I felt. Nothing else mattered. The lifelong looks, stares, jokes, teasing and the all the feelings of weirdness were drowned in the pulsating beat of the music. I finally felt like I belonged somewhere. I could have danced in that same spot forever, and then Tonie invaded my personal space from behind. All the irritations I felt toward her had subsided by the music, a couple of sips of a blue drink, and the comfort of belonging somewhere.

X4

Tonie and I became a couple after that, but it didn't last more than a few months. Her drinking and temper were a constant issue. Not only that, but she had spent the night in my room one night when my roommate was out of town. I got up to go to the bathroom the next morning, and when I returned, Tonie was gone. The covers were pulled up, but the bed wasn't made. I started to straighten the covers and felt a wet spot. I snatched the covers back, and there was this huge pee spot in my bed. I knew it wasn't me. My clothes weren't wet, and I had just gone to the bathroom. This heifer had peed in my bed. Was this college or daycare? I was furious, and then she had the audacity to just leave and not say anything. Oh no, I was done. She was a pissy, temperamental drunk, and the saddest part was that she had not been drinking any alcohol the night before—at least not that I know of anyway.

I snatched the covers off my bed and started fussing at her in my head. *You pissed in my bed and left without saying a word. You could have said something, anything. Big grown wannabe a man and still pissing the bed! What kind of *&$@# is that? Where do you get off wanting to be in control and can't control your own bladder?*

I was furious as I went to the bathroom to fill a pan with some water to scrub the mattress. Since this was a dorm mattress, it wasn't a cloth cover but more like a vinyl cover, but it still needed scrubbing because of the smell. My roommate would return and think it was me since she wouldn't have known I had company. I really didn't care about what she thought right now, especially considering I had found a used condom in my trash can when I returned from out of town

40

one weekend. Why didn't she just tell her boyfriend to put in in her trash can? Why would you put it in mine? So you can advertise? Like I actually cared whom you laid up with. The more I thought about my roommate's trifling attitude and Tonie's inconsiderate ways, the more I began to question myself as to why I even was being bothered with a female. I didn't dwell on that thought too long. I enjoyed the feeling. I enjoyed the closeness, the knowing. Oh hell, to be honest, I enjoyed the sex.

The sex was different, of course, but it was enjoyable—something I hadn't enjoyed after being fondled as a little girl by men with perverted hands, molested in my sleep, forced to have sex with boys I didn't want to have sex with, violated, lied to, contracting STDs, and assaulted. I had grown to dislike men and what they represented. Now this relationship—or whatever this was with Tonie—didn't feel all that great either. Maybe I just picked the wrong one, or maybe the wrong one picked me. I realized that what I was attracted to initially with her was outweighed negatively by all drinking, cursing, the jealous tirades, the insecurity, and now her *pissing in my bed*! "Goodbye!" was all I gonna say. I wasn't dealing with this. I scrubbed and dried the bed as best I could. I got a towel and laid it across the wet spot and then got my iron and turned it up high without steam and ran it back and forth on the spot. I took the sheets and all my covers and took them down the hall to the laundry room to wash them. I felt a calm coming over me after I decided to just call it quits with her. After a couple of hours, I had finished cleaning up the mess Tonie made in my bed. I knew I needed to go clean up the other mess and talk to her.

I made my way across campus to her dorm. I knocked on her door, and she opened it and just stood there looking at me like "You want something?"

"We need to talk," I said.

"I already know what about, and I don't want to hear it" was all she could say, and she stood in the doorway like she didn't want me to come in.

"Can I at least come in? I don't want to stand here in the hallway talking." I was irritated already, and she wasn't helping at all, especially since this was all her fault. Yes, I had a part in it, too, but I didn't make her piss in my bed. She stepped to the side.

"Suit yourself, but I *don't* want to hear it," she said again with emphasis, like she wasn't in the mood to talk.

Oh well, pissy, I thought, *you are hearing it.*

I stepped in and closed the door behind me. I noticed she had changed her clothes and wondered if she had even bothered to take a shower. I had all these thoughts in my head earlier, but now I didn't know what to say to her. She had that same wounded look on her face, but I wasn't falling for it. She wore that look, I came to realize, to make me feel sorry for her and change my mind plenty of times before when she had done something I didn't like and made me mad at her.

Not this time, pissy. For some reason, I wanted her to explain. I felt like she owed me that much. "So you are not going to say anything about what you did or why?" I asked.

She shrugged her shoulders and looked at me, and just like that, the wounded look was gone. And I saw the anger building.

"What do you want me to say? You came over here and said you had something to say, so say it," she said, inching closer to me as she said it like she was stepping up to a fight. I was beginning to see I was right and that this had to go. I didn't like fighting, and I didn't instigate drama. But I would defend myself at all costs and with whatever I could pick up and use.

"I want you to say why you pissed in my bed and left without saying anything," I said. "That would be a good start." I waited for her to respond.

"Are you sure it was me?" she questioned me as if it had been me.

"Really? I know it wasn't me, and the fact that you still can't admit it tells me there is a problem that you don't want to deal with," I responded, feeling the anger rising in my chest and showing in my voice.

"Is that what you came to talk to me about? I really don't want to talk about it. So if that's all you have to say, then you can just leave," she said as she waved her hand to dismiss me and turned and walked away from me.

"No, that's not all I want to say." I took a deep breath and just let it run out my mouth. "I can't do this anymore. I want out." The words weren't all the way out of my mouth before she had me jacked up against the door. Her eyes were full of meanness, and the magnetic smile became a growl.

"So you just gonna leave me! Just because of that? You're just like everybody else. They all say the same thing!" she said while tightening her grip.

I knew it would come to this. All the signs had been there. If I wanted out, I was going to have to fight my way out. I just looked at her.

"Whatever you are going to do, do it. It's not going to change how I feel or my decision. I don't care anymore. You can beat me, choke me, whatever is in your mind. Do it!" I dared her.

I wanted it to be over, and if it came with a fight, so be it. She shoved me harder into the back of the door and then threw me on the bed. I ended up on my back with her standing over me. She lunged forward and hit her fist on the bed beside my head. I just looked at her, not with fear, but with pity. When someone wanted to leave a relationship, this type of behavior only confirmed that decision. I pushed her off me, and she didn't fight me on it.

"Just go. I don't need you. I don't need anybody," she said as she hung her head in her hands. I felt bad for her but not bad enough to stay.

"Bye," I said, and I left out the room.

On the other side of the door, my heart started racing. I didn't know if I was hurt or angry. What I did know was that it was over and there was no going back.

A short time after that, I ran into Tonie's cousin Carla on campus. She asked me how things were going, and I told her what happened. I did leave out the pissy part. Even though I didn't owe Tonie anything, I would spare her that embarrassment. Carla said she wondered how long it would be before I saw Tonie's true colors. She said they were related and all but they were totally opposite in behavior. She gave me her number and said to call her if I ever needed to talk.

That "if I ever needed to talk" came sooner than I expected. I had been so wrapped up with Tonie that I had isolated myself from pretty much everyone else I knew. The phone calls with Carla eventually led to other things. I asked her if she felt bad considering I had been with her cousin.

"Her loss is my gain. No love lost. She knows how it goes," Carla said like she really didn't care what Tonie would think. I didn't care either.

Carla was just the opposite of Tonie in every since of the word. She didn't drink, and she didn't curse like a drunk. She wasn't as nonchalant or moody. She took me home to meet her mother, and they had a good relationship. The days passed a lot quicker, and the school year was coming to a quick end but not before I lost in the "lottery."

The lottery was where first-year students were given housing on campus since on-campus housing was limited. At the end of the year, however, your name was drawn to see if you would continue to stay on campus. I didn't get to stay on campus, so I would have to find a place to stay when I returned.

I found a job at a chicken plant for the summer and stayed with my aunt in Hinesville, which was also where Carla lived. So that worked out pretty well. We hung out on weekends when I wasn't working and went out to the clubs quite regularly. On one our many trips to the club, we ran into some friends of hers that were from Statesboro, where we went to school. They were not in school, but I felt awkward in the presence of Tammy. She was flirting with me, and I knew it. I tried not to make eye contact with her, but I could feel her staring at me. Carla wasn't paying it any attention. I chose not to say anything because I actually felt an attraction toward her. She was cute with very soft eyes and lips that looked like they were naturally wet. Unlike Carla and her cousin Tonie, Tammy couldn't pass for a boy even if she tried. I felt myself getting heated just looking at her eyes whenever I did glance at her.

I better keep my distance, was all I could think.

Carla and I left the club together, but my mind was not on her. I felt like I had fallen into the eyes of a complete stranger.

The summer came and went, and when I returned to college, I had found a place to stay off campus. My brother and I decided to share a mobile home not far from campus. It was the perfect arrangement. I now had the freedom to have over whom I wanted without having to explain or hide from my roommate. The only glitch was that my brother didn't know I was into girls. However, his classes, work schedule, and ROTC obligations kept him gone most of the time.

On one of those occasions when he was away, Carla and I decided to have a small get-together. I suggested that she invite a few of her friends over and we could have a small house party. I didn't want to seem to anxious, but when she mentioned she would invite Tammy and a few others, I felt my heart leap for joy. Everyone showed up, and it was quite an interesting night. We played cards, drank a few beverages, and lip-synced like we were on stage at the club. By now I had advanced to drinking wine. Boones Farm was my favorite. The party came to a weird halt when my brother showed up with one of his friends. I thought his bighead butt was out of town.

He plopped down on the couch and smiled when he said. "Now this is what I am talking about—a room full of women!"

I wanted to just fall on the floor and ask him how with all those brains that he had, he couldn't see for looking. One of Tammy's friends began to croon along with the Donny Hathaway song "Singing This Song for You." She stood up and began dancing for everybody, and here came Mr. Smarty again.

"Who she supposed to be—Marvin Gaye?"

Well, you got one part right, I thought to myself. Finally, I had enough and leered at him. "Hey, don't you have somewhere else you can go instead of intruding in on our party?"

"So you kicking me out my own crib?" he asked.

"Not kicking you out. Just requesting you to remove yourself from the scenery. This is an all-girls party," I answered.

"Whatever. Y'all lame anyway. We can go where some real interesting women are! Let's go, man." He went in his room and grabbed an overnight bag and left with his buddy.

Good riddance. Now we can back to being ourselves. That was what we did—laughing, singing. And of course, the entire night, Tammy and I flirted with each other. As the night wound down to a close, one by one each person said their goodbyes. On the way out the door, Tammy hugged Carla and then came toward me.

"I'm not gonna hug you. I'll just shake your hand," she said to me with a smirk.

I was wounded when she said it until I felt a small wad of paper in my hand. I held it tight between two fingers. I didn't want to put it in my pockets because I knew Carla was going to be touchy-feely as soon as they left since they were the last ones to go. As soon as the door closed, she was up on me.

"Hold that thought. I have to pee," I said and darted quickly to the bathroom. I unfolded the wad of paper, and my heart fluttered when I read it.

It said, "I think you're sexy. Call me."

I quickly memorized the number and flushed the paper down the toilet. I couldn't wait until the next day to call the number since Carla had already made plans to spend the night. I wanted to tiptoe out the bed that night so many times and call Tammy, but I decided against it. I would wait. I began to rationalize in my mind and sort through the details. It wasn't like I had really made it official with Carla. Yes, I did care about her and enjoyed our time together, but I wasn't and didn't feel the butterflies or the tingling when I thought about her like I felt with Tammy. Carla had gotten me past the Tonie phase, but once that was done, I felt like I was just there. I finally dozed off and woke up with excitement, something I hadn't felt in a long time.

I had to get away from Carla somehow today. Yep, got it—my period. It was coming on early. That was my story, and I was sticking to it true or not. It was a good way to run her away. I eased out of bed and went to the bathroom, opened up a pad, and put it on. I stayed in the bathroom a while to help the story along. Just like clockwork, the knock at the bathroom door came about fifteen minutes later.

"You all right in there?" I heard through the door.

"Nooooooo, I got my monthly visitor," I said as if I were writhing in pain.

"Ughhh. Already? You're early!" she said.

"You don't have to tell me. I know that part already. Must be all that wine I drank last night," I responded, still feigning pain.

"You need anything?" she asked.

I want to say, "Yeah, for you to leave." I decided against it and just told her, "Nothing, just to lie down."

My period was a beast whenever it did come on—severe cramps, diarrhea and bad headaches. Sometimes it was to the point where all I could do was stay near a bed or a bathroom the first few days. She had been around for a while enough to know how it would go. I ran the water and washed my face and opened the door with the saddest look on my face.

"Ewwwwwwww" was all I heard when I opened the door.

I pushed past her and crawled back into the bed and pulled the covers over my head. I heard her go use the bathroom and come back and flop down on the bed. She peeped her head under the covers, and when she did, I gave her the evil look.

"Well, I think I am going to head back home and let you get some rest. I know you don't want me holding your hand right now," she said with a sad look on her face.

I should have felt bad, but I didn't. I was waiting to hear that. I snatched the cover back over my head and didn't say anything as I turned my face in the opposite direction. She lay there a while, waiting for me to respond. When I didn't, she got up and put on her clothes and said she would call me later and check on me.

"Lock the front door behind you, please," I told her without looking up or moving.

Hinesville was about an hour away, so I knew that once she got there, she wasn't going to drive all the way back just see how I was doing. As soon as I heard her car crank and the sound of it move farther away, I was up and heading toward the phone. I dialed the number I had committed to memory, and a voice I didn't recognize as Tammy answered the phone. I tried to sound very professional in

47

case I had created tension calling this early. My mother always told us not to be calling folks house early or late at night.

I politely asked for Tammy, and the person dropped the phone and yelled, "Tammy, pick up the phone! It's for you!" There was a slight pause and then "I don't know. Pick up the phone, and you will see."

I heard another phone being picked up and one hung up. The next voice I heard made my heart melt.

"Hello?" she said, unsure of whom the hello was for.

"Good morning! This is Lane. I am following the directions from your note. You said to call. I hope it's not too early and I didn't wake you," I said all at one time.

"Nooo, of course, not." She giggled. "I am glad you called. I was wondering if you would be able to manage that with your security guard right there," she said, laughing.

I could see her smiling through the phone with those always-wet lips and beautiful smile. What was it with me and teeth?

"I figured out a way. We're cool and all, but I am not all they way there like she would want me to be. I mean, she is the second stud that I have been with, but if I am going to be with someone who thinks they are a man, I may as well be with one. That's just my thoughts."

"Well, why are you still there then?" she asked.

"Waiting for someone like you," I returned without even thinking.

"So not only are you sexy, but you're quick. That sounds like something you have said before," she said.

"No. You're the first. There was something in your eyes that just drew me in—the way you carry yourself and the fact that you don't look or act the part. You are just you," I said, being truthful.

"Well," she said, "we will see. What are you doing the rest of the day?" she responded.

"Nothing, I pretended sick to get alone," I said.

"So you lied, but you want me to believe what you just said to me," she said before she laughed.

"The choice is yours. I know I like what I see, and I know you do as well. If not, you wouldn't have given me your number.

It's not like I asked for it. So apparently you were ready to get with me regardless of whether I was a liar or not," I said with assurance in myself and waiting for the phone to be hung up after my smart mouth just popped off.

"Yes, you are quick. I like that. I would love to see you today. I have to go to work. Maybe you could come through, and we can talk some more."

"Yes, I would love that. Tell me the place and the time, and I will be there," I said.

"Say, around one o'clock at Mark's Car Detail shop on Main. Do you know where it is?" she asked.

"I will find it and you," I said without missing a beat.

"Yeah, you are good," she said, laughing. "See you then."

I begin kicking and shouting when I hung up the phone. I felt like a little schoolgirl with a first crush. I checked the clock. I still had about four hours. I had to wait until I knew Carla was home. She would be calling to check in when she got there. I mulled around in my head what to wear and what to say. This was weird in a weird kind of way. I had totally gotten beyond Michelle, Tonie, and Carla—all within one phone call, all with no remorse, no regrets or afterthoughts.

About an hour later, the phone rang, and it was Carla. I answered as if I really didn't want to talk. I really didn't want to talk. She told me she had made it home and that it was a good thing that she went home. Her brother was bringing her nephew over, and she was excited to be able to spend time with him. She began to be chatty about that and a few other things, and I listened with one ear and one-third of my mind. I looked up at the light fixture and frowned at the amount of dust that had collected around it.

"Helloooo? You still there?" I heard her in the middle of my dust gazing.

"Yeah," I lied. I wasn't there mentally or emotionally.

"Well, I'ma let you go so you can get some sleep since you not talking. I will call you later. I love you," she said and waited for a response.

"Yeah, I love you too. Later." I lied again. Well, not really. I did love her but not the way I was supposed to or the way she felt about me. I was unsure of what I wanted and whom I wanted. I got the whole idea about the stud with a fem. I understood that part, but I didn't agree with it. A stud, a manly woman, was typically with a woman who was more feminine, typically. I didn't totally agree with that. If you were woman and you were attracted to a woman, then that was the part. Why be with a woman who pretended to be a man? You might as well be with a man. I was confused and confusing myself the more I thought about. Either that, or I was trying to excuse myself for what I was feeling and thinking toward Tammy. If she and I were out together, no one would suspect anything or stare as if we were disfigured. I had to figure all this out somehow. My time in college was winding down. I was in my junior year and on track to graduate by June 1991. I had the remainder of this year and the next school year to figure it out and decide what I was going to do professionally and personally.

I was working on my degree to become a teacher, and there were just some things that were frowned upon, and my being with a woman would be one of them. Not to mention my mother would kill me. What about my family? Those two thoughts alone made me jump out of bed and take a shower. I only had a couple more hours until I saw Tammy, and I wasn't going to spend them with these thoughts. I knew this was different. I was excited just thinking about her without any physical contact between us. I was drawn to her in my heart and my mind. I was in love with a woman that I didn't even know.

Wow. The answer finally came. That was maybe what love at first sight was all about, even with a woman. Yes, I had been attracted to the others for one reason or another, but this thing with Tammy was running deep, even to the point where I was lying to someone who cared for me. I felt bad for a quick second and then shrugged it off.

Oh, well. I can do what I want. I am twenty-one years old. That makes me an adult.

Actually, I hadn't been twenty-one long.

It was just a month ago. I had celebrated it with Carla and a quart of MD 20/20 or best known as Mad Dog 20/20. I found out that night why it was called such a name. I consumed the entire quart by myself and could only recall leaving the club with Carla and puking my guts out after we got to the hotel room. That was the drunkest night of my life and the last time I would ever drink that purple gasoline in a bottle. Yes, I celebrated being twenty-one in royal fashion, so I didn't have to answer to anyone about my decision. I had one mother, and she was the only woman I answered to about what I did and when. Now that I was twenty-one, that was going to be limited as well.

I turned up the radio to help drown out the thoughts and calm my nerves as I found something to wear. I felt like I was going on a first date. "Poison" by Bell Biv Devoe was blasting, and I started dancing and getting excited. How appropriate for this occasion! I had been poisoned by Tammy. I put on the tightest jeans I had in order to show off my curves. I had been told that I made a pair of Levi's talk to whoever was behind me. So I gazed back at the mirror as I said, "You're welcome." I checked the clock, and it was almost time. A few squirts of perfume, and I was out the door. As I was driving, I wondered what to say.

Just be yourself and be truthful. You have told enough lies to Carla. That's the plan.

I arrived at the detail shop, and the guy looked at my dark-blue '81 Maverick and frowned. It was old but clean and in good condition with no dents, rust, or scratches, so I didn't know why he was frowning. I told him I was looking for Tammy, and he pointed toward the rear near the detail area. As I walked toward the back, I saw her pushing a shop vac toward a car. When she saw me, she smiled and shook her head as if in disbelief. Even in work clothes, she was cute and made my heart race.

"Well, you showed up, I see," she said, smiling with her lips still looking as if she had just licked them.

"Any reason why I wouldn't?" I asked.

"Not sure right now, but I'm glad you did," she replied. "So what's the plan now?"

"Plan for what? For the rest of the day or for the moment?" I was unsure of the question.

She laughed again, and I was just mesmerized by the sound of her laugh and the ways her eyes and lips looked wet and dreamy. I was gone, and I knew it. Judging by the way she continuously flirted with her eyes, she knew it as well.

"I am ready for whatever you are ready for," I said.

"Be careful what you ask for. You may not be able to handle all this. I ain't no rookie," she said with a smile on her face.

"That's what I am counting on," I said without cracking a smile and staring directly into her eyes.

"Well, let's get this party started," she said and threw a rag at me. "Did you come to look, or you gonna help?"

"I don't want to get you in trouble on your job," I said, hoping I wouldn't have to leave. I didn't care what she was doing. I wanted to do it with her.

"Boss man don't mind, as long as he don't have to pay you," she said and laughed again. I grabbed the rag and helped out where I could, drying or vacuuming and talking when we could.

After a couple of hours, the work came to a slow crawl, and her boss said that was it for the day. She told me to follow her to her sister's house, where she was staying. She introduced me to her sister and said she was going to shower and change. I sat in the living room waiting, and her sister begin to drill me, asking me the regular—how old I was, where I was from, what I was in school for, where I lived, if I had a job, where I worked, how long I had known Tammy, where I met her, and all. I got the impression that her sister already knew about Tammy's attraction to women, and she was cool with it. She just wanted to see what was going on.

I thought to myself, *I am in college, and your sister works at a car wash. I definitely ain't using her, and she can't use me. So what's the big deal? Mind your own business.*

I was relieved when I saw Tammy came out all fresh and clean. She could have kept on what she had on. I wouldn't have cared. She was beautiful, and I was stuck on stupid for her. She looked at me as if she knew what had happened while she was in the shower.

"Don't worry. My sister's harmless and nosey," she whispered in my ear but loud enough for her sister to hear.

The look on her sister's face confirmed what I suspected. She knew, and she didn't care. She dismissed us with a wave of her hand and said, "Whatever." We both laughed as we walked out the door. Finally, after waiting all day, I would be alone with her.

"Where to?" I asked, already hoping the answer would be "Your place."

"Your crib, unless that's a problem," she said with a wanted-to-know look on her face.

"Not for me, unless my brother is there. I don't want him in my business," I said, and she laughed as if I had made a joke, but I was drop-dead serious. "What's so funny?" I asked.

"Nothin', but you say that like he don't already have a clue. Trust me. He has thought about it but not actually admitted it," she answered.

"No, he doesn't have a clue, and I am not trying to give him any. I don't want him or any of my family to know. Not right now. I don't think my mother could handle it," I responded, getting a little annoyed with the topic. I didn't want to talk about it, but it would be a problem if my brother was there. I didn't want to have to explain or answer any questions from him. All of a sudden, my being grown started to dwindle away, and I was feeling like a small child having to answer to all my folks. I wanted to change the subject and quickly.

"So what's the plan when we get there?" I steered away from that irritating water into something more pleasant.

"You're slick, but not that slick. If you don't want to talk about it, just say so. At some point, you are going to have to be comfortable with who you are, and so will everyone else. The plan is to show you how to be comfortable."

That ten-minute ride went quicker than I realized, and I couldn't get that li'l blue Maverick in the yard quick enough. I was more than relieved when my brother's car wasn't in the yard. I exited the car and looked around as if I were about to break in my own house. I felt guilty, but I felt excited and wonderful all at the same time. It was a different feeling unlike any I had felt before. She was the honey, and

I was a fly with my wings stuck in her syrupy liquid. As we headed to my bedroom, I was beginning to believe she was the fly with her six hands all over me. After I closed the door, she pulled me to her. Then pushed me on the bed. Now I was confused all the more. She was very feminine, more so than I was, but she was very aggressive. Who cared? I was enjoying how she made me feel. When she went down, yep, I was done. Yes, this was the one! I believed I saw stars in broad daylight. I couldn't explain, and even after we both lay there, panting and dry-mouthed, I wanted more. But somebody wanted a cigarette.

"You smoke?" I asked with a surprised look on my face.

"Yes, I do! Is that a problem?" She looked dead in my face with those adorable eyes and too-wet lips.

"Not a problem, as long as it's outside, please. I don't want the smell in my room or in my clothes," I responded.

"Okay," she said and jumped out the bed and put on her clothes, and so did I. We went out the back door right by my bedroom door and sat on the steps as she smoked her cigarette. Even the way she smoked looked sexy, and I had no desires to smoke a cigarette. I had tried it once when I was in ROTC at my previous college. Tina told me it would help calm my nerves before I repelled down the side of Mt. Conyers. We had gone there for a "real army" experience for three days and two nights. I took a couple of pulls of the cigarette that night and went down the side of that mountain in the dark. The cigarette didn't calm my nerves or help my breath. Worst taste in my mouth ever. Worse than the leaves we used to roll up as kids and light to pretend to be smoking. No, thank you for the cigarettes. Tammy made them look appealing, but I couldn't get past that smell.

When she finished, she tossed her cigarette butt in the air and just stared at me. I knew there was a question coming as she formed her mouth around the words.

"So what are you going to tell your friend Carla?" She finally spit it out.

"Tell her about what?" I asked, getting irritated at the thought.

"About the price of tobacco! What do you think? Don't play dumb. You can't have both, and from the way you look at me, she will pick up on it when she's around," she said.

54

She was right. I couldn't hide it. I wasn't very good at hiding my emotions, and I wasn't a good liar. I either told on myself or confessed to what I had lied about.

"I will deal with it when I have to. Right now I'm not thinking about that or her. It's not like I'm in love. I care about her, and I am pretty sure if and when I do tell her that it will hurt, but I'm just not into her like she is with me," I said, getting a knot in stomach just thinking about it. She sure was slowly killing the mood. "I will deal with it, just not right now."

She cut her eyes at me and said very slowly, "I don't like to share."

The seriousness of the words made me realize at that moment that I had to make a decision. If I took too long, then Tammy would be gone. If I rushed and told Carla and things with Tammy didn't work, I was all alone. They called this "the life." It sure was complicated. I hung my head in confusion and despair. Before I knew it, she was in front of me and lifting my chin and winking her eye.

"I ain't going nowhere, not right now. Just figure out what you want to do and let me know. I don't want to be second to anyone, and I understand this is all new to you, so I will give you some time," she said, and then she turned and went inside. She went in the room and started putting on her shoes. I was disappointed and saddened immediately.

"So I won't be able to see you anymore?" I asked with my heart pounding, waiting for an answer.

"Yes, but not like this," she said, pointing toward the bed, "not until you have handled your business."

My heart felt like it weighed a ton as soon as the words spilled from her sexy lips. I wasn't prepared for that. I felt my eyes begin to water, and I fought the drops back. I would not act like a baby, even though at that very moment, I felt like curling up in my mother's lap with my head on her shoulders. I put my shoes on slowly, hoping the answer would change or she would say, "Just joking!" Neither one of those happened. The drive back to her sister's house took longer than it did earlier. There was very little conversation. As a matter of fact, there wasn't any. I felt the water welling up in my eyes the closer we got to her sisters. When I pulled up to the front door, she grabbed my hand and winked her eye and jumped out the car. Before she closed the door, she looked back inside the car and told me to call her. The door closed, and the dam that had been holding the water broke. I drove home as best as I could. It wasn't raining outside, but all the rain inside the car from tears was making it difficult to see.

By the time I made it home and flopped down on my bed, I knew what I needed to do. I just didn't know how to do it. I wanted to be with Tammy, and even though she didn't want to share, I never thought about doing that. I just didn't realize it would be so soon. I knew I wouldn't see Carla for another week. I could easily dodge her doing the week with classes and the phone calls.

I spent the week going to classes, talking to Tammy on the phone, and visiting her on her job. The more time I spent with her, the more time I wanted. I talked a couple of times to Carla. As always she was so occupied with her environment and being so chatty she never noticed that I wasn't talking that much. By that Friday, I was certain I was making the right decision. I talked to Tammy that night and told her I had made my decision. I was going to tell Carla when she came on Saturday. She told me to call her after I finished talking with her.

Saturday morning came, and I started doubting again, wondering if I was making the right decision or not. I didn't have any friends I could go to for advice. Nobody knew about my choice in women, so whom was I going to tell? I couldn't call my sisters. They didn't know, so I decided to follow my feelings and tell Carla it was over or whatever it was that we had been doing could not continue. I could have just picked up the phone and called her, but for some reason, I wanted to tell her in person. I didn't know why, I just did.

By the time she showed up that afternoon, I had just about lost all my nerves. She came in her usual jolly fashion, talking about her nephew and wanting to hug me and laugh and giggle. I must not understand this really. On the outside, she looked every bit of a dude, but her attitude and even her sometimes squeaky voice told another story. After about a hour or so, she final noticed that I wasn't really there in thought and decided to ask me what was wrong with me. I felt a golf ball in my mouth, which I tried to swallow before I could say anything.

"We need to talk" was the only thing I could get out.

"We've been talking already, silly," she said as she gave me a slight shove on my shoulders.

"No, not like that. I mean really *talk*." I put emphasis on the word *talk* and said it very slowly as though I were defining the word for her. As soon as I said it that way, her face drew serious, and she looked at me as if she could see what I was about to say.

"Who is it?" she asked very quickly. "Who you been with?" was asked before I could even answer the first.

I stood up and tried put some distance between her and me. The last thing I wanted was to be sitting next to her and tell her it was her friend. Then I got bold in my thoughts and said to myself, *Why should she be upset? She did the same thing to her cousin with me. Who is she to be so judgmental about somebody else? I* didn't have much time to process much because before I could say anything, she stood up and was in my face. I backed away, only to have her grab my arm and pull me back.

"Look," I said, "don't pull on me. I am trying to talk if you would let me finish! I didn't say I had been with anybody. I just can't do this no more with you!" I spit it out as fast as I could before the golf ball formed in my mouth again.

She looked at me, and she knew I was lying about being with somebody else; but she also knew I was telling the truth about not wanting to be with her anymore. When the reality of the truth set in, she jacked me up against the wall. I managed to wriggle myself free and run to the bedroom with all attempts to lock the door. Before I could manage to get the door closed, she burst through the door like a rampaging bull, knocking me back on the bed. I couldn't get up. Then she came down on top of me and sat on my stomach and pinned my hands above my head. She cursed me for every minute that she had spent with me. She was mad and hurt. It was a terrible combination with me pinned underneath it all. I told her I was sorry, that it just happened. Why did I say that?

"So you have been f——n' someone else? Who? I don't even need to ask. You don't know anybody but..." she said furiously, with spit flying everywhere. As soon as she got to the *but*, her eyes grew wide, and she got so close to my face our noses touched. "Tammy? That's who you f——kin'? You so stupid! She don't care nothing about you. I knew it! I knew it! I saw how she was looking at you at the party, but I said, 'Nah, you wouldn't.' I trusted you! And you want to shake me for that?"

I started to say something, but she told me to shut up. She didn't want to hear anything I had to say. "Get off of me!" was the only thing I could grunt out with her on top of me. She was twice my size and a lot stronger than I realized.

"I am not getting up till you say it!" she growled.

I could only close my eyes and turn my face away from hers, and when I did, I felt a stinging pain on my cheek. I realized after the pain increased that she was biting me—not a loving bite, but like she was about to take a plug out my cheek. I started screaming to the top of my lungs. I didn't care who heard me—the neighbors, the trees, the store two miles away. Finally, she turned me loose. Yes, I had made the right decision. This girl was crazy.

Whatever made her do that must have left her body immediately because when she saw the results of her teeth, she apologized and said it was all my fault. My cheek was stinging like someone had poured alcohol on a open sore.

She stood up and started talking to herself. "See what you made me do! I love you, and then you do this to me with somebody that don't even care about you!"

I sat up on the bed, crying as I put my hand to my cheek. I could feel the indentations from her teeth in my skin. I didn't feel any blood, but I felt the pain. I turned my head toward the mirror and saw the color of my light-brown skin darkening in the indented circle.

"You have less than five seconds to leave before I call the police," I said as calmly as I could so that she would understand I wasn't playing.

"I will leave, but you will be back. When she has dogged you out and hurt you, you will be back," she said.

"Three," I said. "You have already wasted the other two." I stood up and started toward the phone.

"I'm out," she said, and she walked away and didn't look back. She was training to be a correctional officer. The last thing she needed was a charge. She was about to get one if she didn't leave my house. The evidence was all over my cheek.

I went the kitchen to get some ice and trying to stop the heat and the pain that was throbbing in my cheek. The heat stopped, but the pain only dulled momentarily. I couldn't believe what had just happened. Then again, yes, I could. She was no different from her cousin—violent and mean spirited. It just took longer for hers to show up. If someone didn't want to be with you, why would you want to scar them and beat them before you leave? And I would like to know how this was supposed to be different from being with a man! I was hurt, mad, and confused all at the same time. I didn't even know how I could face Tammy with this tattoo of her teeth on my jaw.

I went to the bathroom and searched for something to put on it. I found some Neosporin and some Band-Aids. I had to use two large ones to cover the area. Not too bad. But I knew there would be questions. I called Tammy and told her I needed to see her to explain what happened. She told me she was headed to her mom's to hang out and told me to come by there and we could talk. I mulled around in my head how to explain, but nothing even close to something that sounded like it made sense came to mind. I could the truth, but even that seemed and sounded crazy.

I dumped her, and she bit me. Yeah, that's really a great novel.

As I pulled up in front of her mom's house, there was a small crowd of folks sitting on the porch. Some I recognized, and some I didn't. Just what I needed—an audience. I spotted Tammy and felt some relief, and then the dread of trying to explain what happened made my stomach start boiling. She waved her hand for me to get out, and I didn't move.

59

I just sat there looking and thinking, *What am I doing? I have had two pyschos. What if this one is another?*

She wasn't manly by appearance at all. She was soft when she spoke, and she had a glitter to her eyes. She couldn't be crazy. She saw I wasn't moving, so she came to the car. When she got around to the driver's side, she saw the reason for my hesitation. She saw the two big Band-Aids and the bloodshot eyes from me crying like a newborn.

She opened her mouth wide as if she was surprised. "Oh my! What happened?" she asked.

"The short version—I told her I couldn't do her no more, she got mad, pinned me down, and bit me," I said.

"Bit you? You mean like a dog bit you?" she asked with a hint of laughter in her voice like that was not the truth.

"Yes, bit me like a dog. Do you need to see the teeth marks?" I responded, getting agitated even more by the thought.

"Oh, wow! She was pissed. Did you tell her why you couldn't do her no more?" she asked, realizing that I wasn't joking.

"I didn't have to tell her. She figured it out," I said, and as soon as I did, her eyes stretched as wide as I had ever seen them.

"You told her it was 'cause of me?" She had a mixed look of fear and anger on her face, like she was more worried about her being bitten next rather than what I had been through.

"I repeat—she figured it out. She knows I don't know anybody like that except you, her, and her cousin. Process of elimination." This conversation was not going like I expected. *So what? She knows it's you,* I thought. Rather than start a different argument with my thoughts, I only responded, "You don't have anything to worry about. She's not coming over here, and she's not going to jump on you. She has too much to lose." That seemed to bring a sigh of relief from her, and then she remembered—I had been assaulted.

"Awwwww, you poor baby, what can I do to make it better? Can I kiss a boo-boo?" she said, laughing.

"No, thank you. I don't want anybody else's mouth on my cheek," I said, shaking my head no.

She told me to get out the car and to come on the porch. They were about to play spades, and I could either play or watch. I really didn't want to be around anyone with my face like this, and she must have noticed.

"You can take the Band-Aids off. It's okay. We all have battle scars. You still look good," she said as she winked her eye and blew me a kiss. I melted right there. Everything that I had gone through that day felt worth it. I felt reassured, and I pulled the Band-Aids off. As soon as I did, her face changed to one of horror.

"She meant business," she said, with no smile or laughter. "You had your tetanus shot?" she asked. "Then again, you may need a rabies shot." She laughed when she said it, and I did the same. That was funny, even in the middle of the pain. I walked with her to the porch, and she announced, "Before any of y'all ask, her ex-girlfriend bit her." Well, that caught me off guard. So much for them not knowing about me. She just put me and all my business out there with her folks. I didn't know how to take that. Their reaction wasn't one of surprise. It was more of "And? Who cares? Let's play cards!"

I sat off to the side of Tammy and watched the first game. Then she asked me to play. I told her I hadn't played that much. She told me to sit down and follow her lead. She would teach me how to play. So I sat, and I was glad I did. The tension subsided during the game, and I felt like I was among family. After winning a couple of hands, I wanted to just be alone with her. She picked up on my signal and told everyone this was our last hand. We won again and stood up. She told them she was tired of beating up on them with a rookie and that we were going for a ride.

We went for a ride—straight back to my place. I felt like a baby lying in her arms, satisfied, full, and loved, unlike the torture I had felt earlier. We talked for a couple of hours, and she said she had work tomorrow and that it was getting late. She was glad that I had taken care of the situation, but she was sorry it resulted in a battle scar. I took her home, and she would call me after she got off work.

The days, nights, weeks, months we spent together after that were indescribable. I felt like I was at the carnival every day. As soon as classes were over, I knew I would have a wild ride with her.

Whatever she wanted to do, we did it. Wherever she wanted to go, we went. I even took her to my mom's house, something I couldn't do with Carla or Tonie. One look at them, and my mother would have known. Tammy didn't look the part. On the outside to everyone, we were just good friends. On the inside, it was something much deeper.

One afternoon, she got off early, and we went back to my house. She wanted to shower first, and she asked me to join her. I went in, dutiful to her requests as always. The shower turned into something else. Then I heard the front door slam. We both looked at each other. I knew my face was one of fear, but hers was more of "So what?"

"Shhhh." I motioned to her. "That's my brother." I listened, and I heard his footsteps coming toward the bathroom.

"Hey, come on out of there. I need to get in there," he said, beating on the door.

"All right, hold your horses. Give me a minute. I just got in here!" I yelled back.

My heart was pounding. I hoped he wasn't going to stand outside the door and wait for me to get out. I didn't hear his size 13s going back down the hallway, so I turned the water back on to let him know I wasn't coming out just yet. Evidently, he got the message, and I heard him stomping back down the hall. Then I heard his door close. I stepped out the shower but left the water running. I signaled for Tammy to come out the shower, and she ran to my room, which was right next to the bathroom. I then turned the water off and went to my room behind her. We were both still soaking wet and dripping water all over the floor. The sight of the water and my wet body must have reminded Tammy where we left off. She pushed me on the bed, and down she went.

Before the moment got too far along, my room door was flung open. I snatched the covers up over us, but it was too late.

"What that girl doing down there?" was all I heard.

"GET OUT!" I yelled at my brother. "Don't you know how to knock?" I was mad. The mood had been ruined, but more so than that, my brother had caught me red-handed. I didn't know what to say or do, and Tammy didn't seem to care about him bursting through the door.

"Oh well, no need to stop now. He has seen us. We may as well finish what we started," she said, heading back to her original position.

"No. Stop." I couldn't. I was embarrassed, afraid, scared, concerned, and mad angry. What if he called my mother? Nah, he wouldn't. He better not! I couldn't think straight. I couldn't do anything else, and that irritated Tammy.

"So how long you gonna keep hiding who you are? It's not like they don't already know," she said, so sure of herself.

"They don't know. Trust," I said, not wanting to entertain the subject at all.

"Who you think you fooling other than yourself? When was the last time you had a boyfriend? When was the last time you took somebody home with you other than your friends, which are all girls? They know. They just not admitting it."

I didn't want to hear what she was saying. I especially didn't want to believe that she was right. I got up and finish drying off and started to put on my clothes. I need to at least try to talk to my brother.

By the time I got my clothes on and made it to the front of the house, he was gone. I felt scared, angry, and worried all at the same time. I didn't know what made him think he could just walk in my room without knocking. Why didn't I lock the door? I thought I had. Apparently, I was in too big of a rush to finish what had started in the shower. I didn't know where he went or whom he would talk to when he got there. What now? What next?

I heard Tammy coming from the back, and this was not what I wanted to deal with right now. She came up behind me and wrapped her arms around me. I felt like melting and hiding all at the same time.

She whispered in my ear ever so softly, "I got you. I am here with you every step of the way. I love you."

The last few words made everything else seem distant and not important. I turned around and looked at her in her face to see it. This was all just words—something said to just make me feel better. The expression on her face was sincere, and her eyes were deep and full of tears. She felt my pain, and I saw hers.

"Well, there's only one thing left to do," she said. "You have to tell it before he does."

"ARE YOU CRAZY?" I pushed away from her and shouted it all at once. "Me? Tell my family? Tell them what? What am I supposed to say?" I asked, still trembling in fear at the very mere thought.

"It won't be as bad as you think. I promise you they already think it anyway. Who can you talk to about anything?" she said as she picked up the telephone from the cradle.

"What's that for?" I asked.

"For you to use and call whoever you can talk to about anything," she said, motioning the phone toward me.

"I can't... I can't do it." I said, shaking my head and sitting down on the sofa.

"All right, I will. What's your sister's number in Savannah? We are calling her," she said, and the way she said it, I knew it wasn't an open-ended option. Part of me wanted to dial the number and just blab it all out, and part of me wanted to stay where I was. She reminded me very quickly that I would rather it come from me instead of my brother. Who knew what he would say? She was right. I gave her the number, and she started dialing. I hoped she was not at home. Just my luck. I heard Tammy say "Hello" and start talking like they were old friends. The very next thing I heard was "Hold on, your sister has something to tell you." The moment between that and me getting the phone felt like forever. I tried saying hello, but my tongue became extremely thick.

"What's up, sis? What's the matter? Is something wrong?" she asked.

"No, I am just calling to talk and see how you feel about..." I stammered.

"She wants to know how you feel about her being with a woman!" Tammy shouted out before I could even finish my sentence.

"Is that what you called me for? Girl, I thought something was wrong." And then she burst out laughing. "I knew it. It knew it! I am about to call your other sister. Hold on!" I heard her click over, and I looked at Tammy.

"I told you they already knew," she said, and she winked her eye at me.

I rolled my eyes at her, but there was an overwhelming relief that I felt when my sister laughed and didn't ask me the thousand questions I had already imagined. The silence on the phone was broken by my oldest sister's voice. I had three sisters and five brothers. I was the fourth oldest, and only one of my sisters was younger than me. Growing up, they always teased me and beat me up and didn't want me around them. They said it was because I was too young. They always left me with my younger brothers, and that was whom I connected with growing up. My sisters didn't like me, and I didn't like them.

After we left my mother's house, we became the best of friends.

"Well, hello, stranger," my oldest sister said. "I hear there's some news you need to share." She was laughing as well.

"From the sound of it, you already heard," I responded.

"Nada only told me parts. I need to hear it from you," she said.

"I have a girlfriend, and you have already met her before." I said. "And that's the news."

"So you mean *girlfriend* as in *friend* or *girl* as in y'all go together?" she asked.

"WE GO TOGETHER A LOT!" Tammy yelled out in the background, laughing as she said it. She had picked up the other phone and had been listening to the conversation. I was glad she was so amused by this conversation because I surely wasn't.

"Oh well, I guess that answers that," she said.

"I told her we already knew. 'Member when we used to tease her all the time about her and her little friends when we were growing up? 'Member how mad she used to get when we said that? We were just joking. We didn't know it was true." She could barely get all the words out between all the giggling and laughing and coughing. My oldest sister Tajuana was laughing so hard I thought she was about to gag.

"Ha ha ha. Y'all so funny," I said.

"Not quite as funny as you are," they said it so quickly together it sounded rehearsed.

"Okay, well, if y'all just want to joke, then I can go," I said.

"Wait, wait, wait! Okay, Nada, get serious. We can laugh later. I want to know what you gonna tell your mother and when are you going to tell her." Tajuana said.

That one question killed the whole joking mood. I hadn't planned that far in advance. I hadn't planned for any of this, and that wasn't a plan I wanted to think about right now.

"I haven't thought about that yet. I will cross that bridge when I get to it," I said.

We continued talking some more as the thousand questions started. The more I talked with them, the more comfortable I felt about myself. They reassured me that they wouldn't say anything to my mother, but they wanted me to let them know before I talked with her. They also told me that that was not something I needed to tell her over the phone. Nada suggested I call and talk to my aunt to get a feel from her as to what route to take and how to approach my mom and dad. This "news" was spreading quicker than I wanted it to spread. The dam had broken when my brother walked in on us.

There was no turning back now or repairing the broken breaches. I didn't want to call my aunt. Even though she was the cool aunt, she was still my mother's sister. We often went and talked to her about stuff that we didn't dare tell my mother about. My sister said she would call her and talk to her and get her to call me. With every person that I had to talk to, it was beginning to be easier and easier, but the very thought of my mother made me shake my head in fear. We talked a bit more, and they said they would call back after they called my aunt.

Tammy came from the back, smiling and clapping her hands. The "I told you so" look was all over her face. I couldn't but laugh at her and with her. I felt safe with her even though she just put all my business out on the front street with my family. I was somewhat relieved, somewhat still hesitant. The battle wasn't over. I still had my mother to deal with and my brother to face when and if he returned home. I was good as long as Tammy was there, winking her eye and holding my hand.

My aunt called me back about an hour later, minus my sisters on the phone. She was laughing and joking like they had been earlier. Her tone was more serious and motherly considering she was more like a second mother than the cool aunt. I didn't feel as comfortable as I had felt earlier. She began the conversation, telling me how she loved me and how much she always the best for me and that hadn't changed. She reassured me that she knew that it was a tough decision for me to open up and talk about it and that whatever support I needed, she was there. After she went back down memory lane and gave me very long "Be sure that this is what you want" speech. She started laughing slightly and said she knew it long before I said anything, so she wasn't surprised. She said the same about my parents. She said they weren't as far removed as I thought.

"So what's the plan? And when are you gonna break the news to them?" she asked without missing a breath between the questions.

"I don't have a plan. This all just came about today. I have thought that far in advance. I am not sure," I said.

"Well, now is as good of a time as ever. The longer you wait, the more stress you will put on yourself. They are more open-minded than you think," she reassured me. "I can be there with you if you think it will help."

"I guess. I can come home this weekend and talk to them. I need to talk to my big head brother here first," I said.

"You haven't told him?" she asked, wondering why.

I explained to her the whole story and how all this came about, with him busting up into my room. She chuckled and said, "Well, I guess that's one way for him to find out."

I told her that he had left before he said anything else. I just didn't want him to tell my mother or anyone else before I had a chance to so do myself. I was trying to give him chance sort it out in his head before I talked to him. He wasn't the friendliest brother I had, and he could sometimes be a butthead.

"He will be okay. He's not a child. Just call me when you get ready to leave and head this way on the weekend. I will see what I can do," she said, and she hung up.

The weight on my chest was getting lighter and lighter. Tammy came and gave me a hug and a kiss on my forehead. She told me she was proud of me and that we could do this together. I told her it was *not* a good idea for her to go with me Saturday. I told her that I would need to face my parents alone. I didn't know what to expect, and I didn't want her to be caught in the middle of what might happen. She said she understood and that she would be waiting to hear from me.

It was late, and this had been very exhausting day. I knew my brother would be back eventually, and I didn't want her there when he did, so I took her back home. I felt free. I felt wanted. I felt loved, and I felt the fear begin to creep in at the very thought of talking to my mother. I wasn't too concerned about my dad. He didn't say much or even have much of opinion about anything.

Anytime I would ask him about something or ask to do something, I would always get the same answer: "Go ask yo' maw." So I had long stopped asking him anything. He didn't go to church much, if any. My mother made all of us go; it was not an option. He was the only one that sat home every Sunday and watched football. I didn't care how much he stayed home on Sundays, though he couldn't go in those pots on that stove and eat before we got home from church. That why probably why we always had to ask her. He knew the rules better than we did.

My brother never came home that night. I was about to leave to go to class the next day when he showed up.

"I need to talk to you," I said. He mumbled something under his breath and then looked at me. His look was cold and empty. "Can you sit down a minute so I can talk to you?' I asked him, trying not to make matters worse. He made a huffing sound before he sat down on the couch.

"Talk," he said. "I don't have all day."

"I want to explain to you about yesterday." As soon as I said so, he leaned back on the couch and closed his eyes as if the memory was still fresh and he wanted it gone. "First off, you shouldn't have just burst into my room without knocking. That was first thing. Second, what you saw is what you saw, and that's who I am," I said it so fast before I had a chance to take it back.

His eyes flew open as soon as I said it. The look in his eyes told me what was coming next.

"So that's something you are going to keep doing? You are telling me that you like women?" The way he said the words and asked the questions made me feel some kind of way.

"Yes, that's what I am telling you, and I don't want you telling Momma or anyone else before I have a chance to tell them," I said, getting defensive.

"You telling Momma this foolishness? Well, I wish you luck with that. You don't have to worry about me telling anybody! I don't like it, and I don't agree with it. I don't want to talk about it. That's your business. Do what you want. I don't want be around it," he said. He stood to his feet and left out the door.

I was stunned but not really surprised. He was a butthead and macho man. All he needed was a buffalo outfit, a large wooden club in one hand, and a woman he was dragging to his cave in the other. His words, as few as they were, made me wonder if I would get the same response from my mother. Born, bred, and fed in the church, she was bound to unleash worse than what my bighead brother just let out. I couldn't worry about that now. I had to get to class. I would worry about that later, like when the time got here. I had a few more days, so it was no biggie.

The time came quicker than I thought. It was Saturday morning before I knew it. I called Tammy to tell her I was leaving, and she said she would see me when I get back and to not worry. Somehow that didn't help at all. I called my aunt to tell her I was on my way. She told me to call her when I got to my mom's and she would handle the rest. The three-and-a-half-hour drive would give me plenty of time to roll around in my head what to say and to prepare my heart for whatever came of the conversations. The ones I had already talked to weren't so bad except the cave man. I hadn't seen him much after that conversation. Maybe he made sure he came and left when I wasn't there. I eased the tension by listening to my cassette player and thinking about Tammy.

In such a short period of time, I had gone from a sheltered life to living on front street. I didn't mind. She made it all worth it.

X5

Winter 1989

I hadn't been home in a few months. The last time I came home, Tammy and a few other friends were with me. Of course, everyone was on their best behavior, so there was nothing out of the ordinary. This trip, I felt different, other than the fact that I was alone and full of hesitation. My daddy was outside, working on a car. He did his usual "What's up?" with his head and went back to work. My mother was more than excited to see me. She and I always had a close connection. My brothers and sisters called me the tattletale because I would tell my mom everything they did when she wasn't at home. That created a bond with her but a distrust with the rat pack.

After I got inside the house, I stole away from her conversation for a few minutes to call my aunt, and she said she would be out shortly and to not say anything until I got there. She said the best route to take would be with my daddy first and then let him break the ice with my mother. It sounded like a good plan to me. I just hoped the ice was the only thing that would be broken.

I went back to the kitchen where my mother was working on Sunday dinner. I decided to help. That way, I wouldn't be so nervous just sitting around. She was preparing a big spread—collard greens, black-eyed peas, green beans (my dad hated them) with potatoes, macaroni and cheese, rice, pig feet, neck bones, baked sweet potatoes, corn bread, and fried chicken. She was putting on the boiling meat, and I was peeling the potatoes for the beans. Her conversation was full of excitement as she told me everything that had happened since I last left. A couple of folks had died that she tried to make me remember, and I didn't know whom she was talking about. About ten minutes into the conversation, I saw my aunt's car pull in the yard, and mother looked surprise to see it; of course, I wasn't. I stared intently at the potato, hoping my look of guilt didn't meet her "Mother knows it all" eyes. She kept at what she was doing and didn't bother to even go see what my aunt wanted.

My aunt never came inside the house, so I knew it was time. I went and peeped out the door and saw my aunt and my dad walking down toward the cane field. My heart started pounding, and there was no turning back now.

A short time later, my aunt came into the house and looked at me and winked her eye. My mother only kept washing the meat in the sink and asked my aunt what she wanted to know when she first saw her car.

"What storm blew you this way? What you doin' out here?" my mom asked.

"Aw, hell, woman, I can't come see my own sister without having a reason?" my aunt shot back. She was always funny to me— smart and smart-mouthed. When her and my mother went at it, they *went* at it. "I heard my niece was home, and I came to see her. I know you will have her stuck out here in this country, and she can't go visit nobody, so I came to see her," she said, and she winked her eye again.

"Oh, you can come see her, but you can't come see me?" my mom asked.

"Nah, you might want me to do some work, and I ain't leaving my house to come work at your house," she said, and she started laughing.

Before my mother could say anything, I heard my daddy call my name, more like yell my name. I thought I had swallowed one of those whole raw potatoes as I walked out the door. He was standing outside in the middle of the yard, looking at me as I walked out. I couldn't tell by his expression whether he was mad or not. He very seldom smiled. When he did, it was a quick smile and then back to the straight face. He had put on a little weight and had his teeth fixed since he stopped drinking and smoking. He looked like a daddy now.

That didn't help me any. All those years had passed. I was no longer in the house to enjoy those daddy moments. This one wasn't going to be easy. He told me to come pass him a wrench. I found it and gave it to him.

"Your aunt tells me you have something you want to say," he said and went back to working on the car.

"What did she tell you already?" I wanted to know before I said anything. He raised back up from the car and just looked at me.

"I'm listening," was all he said, and I knew I had better start talking quickly.

"I have a girlfriend" was all I could get out.

He stood looking at me and just shook his head. He bent down to work on the car and paused. He stood back up and then wiped his hands on a rag. He said in a very calm voice, "It's just a phase you will grow out of it. I'ma tell you this, and maybe one day you will grow to understand it. Whatever the reason why you think you doin' what you doin' really ain't the reason why you have one. You may be mad at your boyfriend or just 'xperimenting. But you'll grow out of it."

"I don't know, Daddy. You're the only man I have ever been around that I really wasn't afraid to be around. You are really the only one that I felt I could even trust."

He let a small smile spread across his face, one that I rarely saw, and told me, "You'll find one. A man gonna always have two women—one that he will love and trust, and the other somebody that don't mean nothing to him. So whatever you goin' through right now, it won't last. What you told yo' momma?"

"I haven't yet. I was hoping you would," I said.

He let out a loud laugh and said, "YOU RECKON?"

"Yes, it might be a little better coming from you," I said.

"That's yo momma. It ain't gon' be no better. I don't care who it come from," he said and went back to working on the car.

"Please," I said and realized that this was probably the longest conversation I had ever had with him.

He rose back up and wiped his hands again. He looked at me, and he must have understood my fear. He started walking toward the house, and as he made it on the porch, my aunt came out the door. They exchanged a few words, and she headed toward her car.

She threw up her hand and said, "See ya later, Flapnanny. I am leaving befo' yo' momma put me to work. I have done my part. Call me befo' you leave and head back."

I could only wave before she jumped in the car and left. I stood there a few moments before contemplating whether I should go in the house or stay outside. I didn't have long to think before my daddy came back outside. Once again, I couldn't read his facial expression. He didn't have one. He came to the car and simply said, "Yo momma want you."

I needed a drink. I needed a cigarette, the ones I couldn't stand to smell, and I needed Tammy. I needed to run and to never look back. I really needed someone to carry me to the porch and up those steps because my feet became heavier with each step. By the time I got to the porch, my mother was coming through the door with a dishpan of greens and a knife in her hands.

"Come help me pick and cut these greens," she said as she sat down in the rocking chair.

My eyes remained fixated on the knife in her hand, and I made sure I sat just far enough away. I kept my head down. I didn't want to look in her face or her eyes. She had a way of knowing just by looking. I picked and stripped the greens, and she rolled them up in her hands and cut them. There were no words said, and I didn't know what to say. My twisting and fidgeting only made matters worse.

"Say it," she said.

"Say what?" I asked, trembling.

"Whatever it is you need to tell me. I always told you that you could talk to me about anything," she said with no anger or coldness in her voice.

I finally raised my head up and looked into her face. She was always so beautiful to me, with her pretty brown eyes, smooth caramel-colored skin, and gorgeous white teeth with that one gold "bling" up front that always sparkled when she smiled. I didn't see that smile right now. I saw a look of concern and thoughtfulness in her eyes. Now she I could read, unlike my daddy. I tried to a least say "I…" but that wouldn't even come out.

"So you done gone the other way?" she asked.

"I guess if that's what you want to call it," I said, not offering any more explanations and holding my head down so as not to look in her face.

"Who showed you that? I know that wasn't how you were raised. I was so afraid when you left here that you would get messed up or caught up in something that you couldn't get out of, but never in my life would I ever thought you would be with a woman. Who approached who?"

"I was approached. I actually didn't want to at first but—"

"Well, you shoulda left it at that," she said, interrupting my explanation. I could see her sitting back in the rocking chair, still cutting greens and her head turned to one side like she was processing it and thinking. "So all them girls you done brought home with you are like that?" She finally asked, and before I could answer, she started naming them one by one. After each name, I would say yes or no. There had only been four of the many that had come home with me that were as she said, "like that." After she had named each one from the last three years that had come home with me, I saw a smirk on her face.

She said, "Humph, that's just something y'all do when y'all get bored."

"No, ma'am, we play cards when we get bored," I said, and when I looked at her face, the look in her eyes cut deeper than the knife in her hands.

"I don't care what you think you are doing right now. I didn't raise you like that. I don't like it, and I don't agree with it at all. You're my child, and I love you. I don't have to love that. That doesn't mean I will treat you any differently. I don't approve of it, but that doesn't keep you from being my child. I can only pray that you will grow out of it. I have a lot more questions, but I will wait. I need to think so more on this. Who else you done told?" she said as if she knew she wasn't the only one.

"Just Tajuana and Nada, and of course, Big Head knows 'cause he is in the house with me."

She laughed and asked what he said. I told her that he wasn't happy at all and that he had been keeping his distance. She reassured me that he would be okay and that everyone was not going to be as accepting as some would be. She told me I shouldn't be surprised if I lost some friends when they found out. That hit a little hard for me. I was beginning to realize that I was being separated from everything that I had already known and entering a whole new world. I could only nod my head that I understood because the reality of what was happening was making my chest heavy.

My mother stopped midsentence with whatever she had been saying and said, "I want you to promise me one thing. I don't care what else you do or who you do it with. Just promise me that you won't ever marry no woman." The tone of her voice told me the only answer she would accept as she stopped cutting the greens when she said it was "I promise."

"Momma, I am not marrying no woman or no man for that matter. I don't even want to be married. Besides, that's not legal anyway," I said as I started back picking on the greens.

"You young. You would be surprised. You just make sho' you don't marry one. That goes against everything in the Bible, including what you are doing. But if you marry one, ain't no coming back from that."

I only understood the "You young" part and nothing else. I really didn't want to understand. I wanted these greens to be finished and this conversation to be over. I had made it through the hardest part, getting it out there for them to know. I guessed Tammy was right. They already knew; they just hadn't acknowledged it. The rest of the green-cutting process was spent in silence, same with the cooking. The truth was, I really didn't understand what the fuss was all about. I knew where my heart was, and I knew where I felt most comfortable. I had relationships with guys that went wrong and the same with females. They all were the same at the end. Hurt was hurt, and abuse was abuse no matter what gender it came from.

I was glad when Sunday came and it was time for me to leave. My mother's mood wasn't as joyous when I left as it was when I came. I wasn't a baby anymore. I was now entering into adulthood to a world unknown to me and forbidden to her. I arrived back home and called Tammy to tell her everything that happened. We talked for a couple of hours, and I was tired and hadn't done any of my homework for class. I told her I would have to catch up with her tomorrow. I needed to study. I wasn't in the books long before my brother came in. He didn't speak. He just went to his room and closed the door. I didn't know how long he was in there, but he came back out with a few bags and sat them on the floor.

"I am moving on campus with a buddy of mine. Maybe you can find a roommate to help you with the rent. I think this is better for both of us," he said with no remorse or emotion.

I just looked at him and then turned my head back to my books, "Your choice. Fine with me." I didn't want him to see me hurt or cry. I didn't think he realized how much his leaving hurt or bothered me. It was if I were contagious and not his own sister. He picked up his bags and said he would get the rest of his things later in the week. I told him to leave the key when he was done, and he walked out the door.

I couldn't focus on the words on the pages of the textbook from all the water that had formed in my eyes. I closed the book and put my head on the table and cried. That was the loneliest moment I had ever felt. I didn't want to talk to Tammy. I wanted to call my mother, and I refused to do that. I didn't want to hear her another sermon from her. I went to bed thinking tomorrow would make today go away.

After a couple of months with school and with Tammy, I was okay. I saw my brother here and there in the cafeteria where I worked, and that was enough for me. I was happy, very happy. My mother began writing me more, and she expressed her concern about someone killing me or beating me in a jealous rage or, even worse, catching AIDs, which was just starting to spread.

Well, too late, for the first two, Momma. I have had a gun in my face twice, been beaten, jumped on, had a few STDs… And guess what, they were all by men.

As far as I knew, I was more prone to catch AIDs from one of them than a woman. At least she didn't have to worry about me getting pregnant. I understood her concern, but I didn't think she really understood everything I had seen or experienced since I had left the sheltered life in her house. I was in a good place, and I was happier than I had ever been.

The Thanksgiving and holiday break would be soon approaching, and I had a decision I had to make. If I left, I would be stuck in the country for the next month and a half and not be able to see Tammy. But since I wasn't staying on campus, I didn't have to leave. I could stay right here in my own place. I just need to find a job to help with the bills since work study was no longer an option. I went back to the chicken plant, and of course, they were always hiring. I only wanted part-time, so that wasn't a problem either.

Right after the Thanksgiving holiday, I called Tammy to see what the plans were for the weekend. She answered the phone and said she couldn't talk at the time and that she would call me back later. However, *later* never came that day or the next. I called her sister when I didn't hear back from her to see if everything was okay, and she told me that I would have to talk to Tammy. I told her that I had been trying but that I couldn't get in touch with her. By day four and no conversation, I decided not to go to work and go to her job and see if I could catch her there since she was always missing in action by the time I got off work and made it home. The next morning, I waited until around her lunch break and drove up to the detail shop. The look on her face when she saw me was one of shock and nervousness.

"What are you doing here? Aren't you supposed to be at work?" she said with a sense of irritation.

"I took off. Where have you been, and why haven't you returned any of my calls?" I asked, getting even more irritated than she appeared.

"I really can't talk right now. Just go home, and I'll call you. I promise," she said with a sense of urgency in her voice.

"You said that the other day, and I still haven't heard from you. What gives?" I wasn't understanding the "I'll call you later." I wasn't understanding anything.

Before she could say anything else, I heard a car horn blowing behind me.

She looked at me and whispered, "Please go. I will call you and explain everything." She then walked away and got in the car that had been blowing the horn. I couldn't see who it was, just a dark outline and long wavy hair.

I went back to my car and sat their motionless, dumbfounded, and unsure about anything that had just happened. I waited, I waited and I waited. The phone call never came. I cried, I screamed, I ached all over, and I felt lost. Did this really just happen? I crawled into bed in the middle of the day, once again hoping tomorrow would come and today would be behind me.

I woke up the next day, and there was snow on the ground. I couldn't even enjoy the beauty of the white freshly covered ground that I loved so much because of all the darkness and pain that I was feeling. I called Tammy's sister and pleaded with her to tell me what was going on. She said she really couldn't tell me but that Tammy would be over sometime that morning and she would make her call me and explain. I wasn't going to wait for that. I threw on some clothes and jumped in my car. Much to my chagrin, it wouldn't crank. I tried, and I tried. Nothing, not even a sound. I would not be defeated. I saw my bicycle, and I was determined to get to the other side of town. I jumped on it. It was difficult at first riding through the snow. I was glad it wasn't that deep. I made it to the highway and was going along rather smoothly for about three miles or so when the back tire went flat. I got off and started pushing it, still headed to the other side of town to get some answers. After about ten minutes of walking, a truck pulled up beside me and asked me where I was headed. I told him where, and he said for me to get in. He was nice enough to put my bike on the back, and he smiled when he got back in and introduced himself. He was an older white guy with hair just as white as the snow. He didn't talk much after he introduced himself, and the last eight miles took just as long as it did for me on my bicycle. When we arrived at Tammy's sister's house, he smiled and got my bicycle off the back of his truck.

"I wish I had something I could pay you for your troubles," I said.

"It was no trouble at all, and you don't have to pay me one dime. I was glad I could help," he said as he hobbled back to the driver's seat and drove off.

I didn't see any other car in the yard but Brenda's, Tammy's sister. I didn't know if I had missed Tammy or not. I knocked on the door, and Brenda opened the door and looked at me in shock. She peeped out the door and looked around as if she were looking for someone else.

"How'd you get over here? I don't see your car," she said.

"My bicycle and a stranger. Where's Tammy?" I wasn't in the mood for small talk.

"She hasn't made it over here yet, but she will be here shortly. Put that bicycle around the back so she won't see it and know that you are in here," she told me.

I did as she said, realizing there was a lot more to this than I knew. When I got inside, Brenda told me to wait in the back room and when Tammy got there, she would bring her back there. She told me that whatever happened or whatever I heard, do not come out of the room. I didn't know what to expect. Why was I hiding like I had done something wrong? I didn't have long to wonder because I heard a knock at the front door. I heard Brenda, Tammy, and another female with a heavy, deep voice that I didn't recognize. They all talked and laughed for about ten minutes, and I heard Brenda tell Tammy to come with her, that she had something to show her. She told the other female to make herself comfortable and they would be right back. I stood back away from the door so I could have a good look when Tammy walked through the door. Brenda walked in first, with Tammy behind her. The look on her face when she saw me was one of horror and fear.

"What the hell? What are you doing here?" she whispered.

"I need answers, and I need them now!" I said.

"Shhh, not too loud!" she said. "I told you I will explain everything."

"When? When you never call like you said. Who is that? Since you can't give me any answers, how about I go ask her!" I said, meaning every word. Before I could even get to the door, they both grabbed me and pulled me back.

"Tammy, you need to just gone and tell her *now*!" her sister said.

"Okay, okay, okay. I didn't know she was coming home. She showed up, and she surprised me. I wanted to tell you. I wanted to, but I didn't expect for things to go as far as they did with you."

"She, she, she—who the hell is *she*?" I was tired of waiting, tired of the dancing. I wanted the truth.

"She's my wife," she said.

When she said it, I remembered what my mother told me while cutting those greens. I couldn't believe it, and I didn't want to.

"Don't be mad, please. I am only going to spend time with her while she is here, and then I am going to tell her it's over. She will be leaving to go overseas, and I won't have to see her. And then it can be me and you. I promise. Just be patient, please."

I really could not process anything beyond "She's my wife." I looked at her, and if I could have gotten away with it, I would have killed her right then. I was beyond hurt. I was in a place I hadn't been with some feelings I didn't understand, and all I know was that where I was at that very moment was all her fault.

"So you have been lying to me this whole time? I told my family because of you. I lost my brother because of you—and a lie that you chose to tell!" I said between the tears as best I could.

"Tammy, come on, let's go!" the voice yelled from the living room.

"I have to go. I will come by and see you tomorrow. I promise." Then she walked out of the door.

I sat on the bed. Brenda put her hand on my shoulder, and then she walked out as well. The tears really began to roll. I felt used, alone, and frightened. I couldn't even call my mother. I couldn't call anyone and tell them how I had been a made a fool. Brenda came back into the room and asked if I was okay. I told her I just wanted to go home. She said she would take me.

The ride back home was longer than I had ever remembered. Brenda talked, but I wasn't listening. I just wanted to get back home and deal with all this information as best I could. She put me and my bicycle out and apologized for her sister. It didn't help. I put my bicycle up and went inside. The house seemed bigger and colder than it had ever been. I was alone with no one to talk to and no one that I wanted to talk to. I went to my bedroom and hated the room now. It reminded me of Tammy. I could smell her in the room. Her picture was on the mirror. I snatched it down and tore it to pieces. Everything on the dresser was destroyed next, then the bed, then the furniture. By the time, I sat down on the bare mattress, my room was a mess. Everything had been turned upside down and reflected my life at that very moment. I didn't want to be here in this room, this house, or this world anymore. I crawled up on the mattress and cried and screamed. No one heard me, and there was no one who cared to hear me.

I didn't know how long it lasted, but when I opened my eyes, it was dark outside. I heard a knock, and I dragged myself to the door. I opened the door, and there she was standing on my steps. She walked right on in like nothing had happened earlier.

"I just came to check on you to see if you were okay. I meant everything that I said. We are going to be together. Just be patient, please." She was pleading.

I just looked at her and walked back to my room. She followed behind me, and all I heard was her gasping and asking, "What happened."

"I couldn't fight you or whoever you were with, so I took it out on the room that reminded me of you," I said.

"Baby, please trust me. We will be together. She will only be here a few days, and then it will be like it was. Just me and you. I can't stay long. I just came to check on you. Please wait and be patient," she said, and she started back out the door. "Oh, and clean up this mess." She giggled as she said it and blew me kiss. I didn't know how I felt at that moment—whether I was happy she came or even more furious.

Trust? Ha! A few days? We will see.

After a few days had passed and I hadn't heard from Tammy, I called Carla and cried. I told her I wanted to die and just be done with all this. She was angry at first and told me not to do anything stupid. She told me to come to her house and just talk.

I agreed and went to her house and cried even more. She said she didn't want to say it, but she told me I was making a big mistake. She knew that Tammy was no good, but I had to learn for myself. She apologized for how we had ended, but it was for the best for both of us. She had moved on and was happy. We could still be friends, and she would be there whenever I needed to talk, but I need to let Tammy go for good. The last part stung a little when she said it, but I knew it was true. I left her house the next day still confused but not suicidal. I at least had a friend that I could talk to when I needed it. A few days turned into a few weeks. By week four, I decided that was enough. I got dressed that Friday night and headed to the club in Savannah. I was in hunting mode, and I needed to put some emotional distance between me and Tammy.

The music was alluring as always. I couldn't drink a lot because I had to make that forty-five-minute drive back. I puffed a couple of cigarettes, another habit I had developed from being with Tammy. I was standing around, just watching all the folks dancing on the floor, when I saw a familiar face. I recognized her as one of the basketball players from college. She wasn't just on the team; she was an awesome point guard with a three-point shot that made you swoon. She was just standing there, watching everyone dance, like I was. I watched her for quite a while to see if anyone approached her or came and stood beside her, marking their territory. After a while, I realized she was there with a couple of other folks from the school, but she was not paired up with anyone. I made my way over and introduced myself. We talked over the loud music for the rest of the night. Before parting, we exchanged numbers, and I told her I would be in touch.

I went home feeling better than I had felt in a while. I wasn't going to drown in Tammy's venom any longer. I was done with her. I went to Bev's basketball practice one afternoon. I stood up on the upper deck of the gymnasium and just watched. She had already informed me that she was a very private person, so I kept at a distance and didn't even let her know I was there. We talked back and forth for a while, and I realized that all these other relationships had never started that way. Her conversations were intelligent and calm. She didn't yell or get angry. She was very mild-mannered and humble. I felt privileged to be in her presence. Eventually, she confessed that she had never been with a woman, that I was her first, but she wanted to share that experience with me. I was blown away. I knew that I didn't want to treat her like I had been treated by those before her, especially that last one. Ugh, not me. Bev had a gentler sweet spirit, one that attracted me to her even more, not because of what I had been through, but because I treated her the way I wanted to be treated. Everything after that first conversation was magical, and I knew that this was the one for me. I was happy, and everything and everybody else was a distant memory.

One month into the relationship, Tammy called and said we needed to talk. I told her there was nothing to talk about. She could keep talking to whomever had kept her occupied for the last two months. I was done.

"So you with somebody else?" she asked, sounding surprised.

"Yeah, so there is nothing else for us to talk about. Goodbye," I said, and I hung up the phone.

The phone rang a few more times after that, but I didn't answer. There was no need to. I knew Bev was at basketball practice, so it wasn't important whoever was calling. I went to back to cooking and cleaning my house. About twenty minutes later, there was a knock at the door. When I opened it, Tammy walked in and pushed me in the chest.

"Oh, so you think it's just that simple? You can just tell me bye, and that will be the end of it? You may as well tell whoever you think you are talking to that you are no longer interested!" she said with the assurance that she still had control. I just stood there looking at here like she was crazier than she sounded. "Answer me! I told you to wait and be patient. But you couldn't wait! So now you need to just get rid of whoever before I find out who it is and do it myself!" she instructed me.

"The only thing that *you can* do is get out my face and out my house! *You* decided to put me on blast with my folks! *You* decided to lie to me over and over and over! *You* decided to make me wait! FOR WHAT! GET OUT!" I was angry. There was no more hurt.

"And if I don't? What are you gonna do? Shoot me with this toy pistol?" she said as she headed toward my pistol that was sitting on top of the TV. My mom had given it to me since I was driving up and down the road a lot by myself. Before she could reach it, I grabbed her and threw her on the sofa. I got to the gun and went to the front door and fired one shot out the door to let her know it wasn't a toy.

"Either you leave or the next one belongs to you," I said, still pointing it out the door. I didn't know that her sister was outside in the car. When she saw me fire a shot out the door, she got out of the car. "If you want your sister, you better come get her and tell her not to come back," I said, and I meant it.

"Tammy! Come on, let's go!" her sister yelled at her without leaving from beside the car door.

"I'll leave, but you'll be back! You won't find another one like me," Tammy said, so sure of herself.

"Yeah, and that will be a good thing," I said and slammed the door and locked it. That part of my life was over, and I was sure of that. I didn't know what plans she had, but I wasn't going to be a part of it.

When Bev called later that night, I told her everything that had happened. She wasn't too happy and said she didn't want no parts of any drama. I assured her that there wasn't. That relationship was over before it started, and she had no worries. She told me she didn't feel comfortable coming to my house right now because Tammy might come back. I told her that she wasn't, but I understood her hesitation, so I didn't push the issue. Tammy didn't ever come back, and I wasn't looking for her to take that chance. I had been pushed to a point where I had never been before, and I didn't ever want to go back.

The rest of the school year and the summer belonged to Bev and me. She went home with me a couple of times, but she hated the country. The last year was both our senior year, and she decided to move off campus with me. The year went by quicker than I had imagined. I had been applying to different schools to teach where I thought we both would be happy. I didn't get any offers except back in my hometown. That was when the fairy tale came to an end. Bev said she was not going there. That the country was a dead-end place, and she had other desires to travel and be in a larger area with something to offer than look at a dirt road and trees. I was hurt. She said she loved me but that she couldn't move there. That was the only place I had been offered a job, and I couldn't just float around somewhere without a job. We both cried and came to a mutual understanding. The relationship was over. With a month left in school, we decided to just cut the ties now before the inevitable came. She moved into the vacant bedroom that had been long left by my brother. It was difficult at first but manageable.

One weekend, we decided to go out, and it was with the under-standing that we were just friends. It wasn't quite as easy as I thought. While we were out, she caught the eye of someone else, and they chatted most of the night. When we headed back, she felt the urge to tell me the conversation. I pretended to be happy and interested, but I wasn't at all. I wanted to tell her to save it for someone else.

Needless to say, that relationship grew closer, and we grew further apart. She did have the decency to tell me that after graduation she had accepted the offer to travel and see the world with her new friend. This new friend was in the military, and Bev was excited to do what she had dreamed of doing. I was happy for her in some sort of weird way. She was a good person and was very loving. She deserved her happiness even if it wasn't with me.

I was back to where I was before she entered my life. Alone. I made the best of the days as I could. I went to the club again, looking for something in a place where there was always somebody else just as lonely. I met her that night, and her name was Carrie. She, too, was military, but she was a little rougher than Bev. I left the club with her that night and went to the hotel with her. I fell for her, and it was very easy. By the time graduation was over, Bev was gone, and Carrie had all my attention. I was good. I met her kids. This was the first relationship that I had been in with someone that had kids. She was a lot older than I, and she was funny. She made me laugh, and that was all that mattered.

I ended up moving back to the country a few weeks after my graduation in June of 1991 to prepare for my new job. I had my own place, right next door to my mother's house in the country. She was glad for me to be home but was hesitant about my life and everyone around there finding out. I really didn't think that much about it. There wasn't anyone there for me, so all my personal affairs would be out of town over four hours away. It was not like anyone was going to come out there in that country and spy on me. Carrie and I continued our relationship, and I went to visit her when I could on the weekends. When I started teaching, the visits were less frequent. About three months in, she told me she was being deployed up north but that we could still continue our relationship. I didn't see any reason why not since I was limited in travel anyway. Our conversations had not changed with the distance, and it was going quite well.

She called me one day to ask a favor. On her next assignment, she would be in the barracks. She said it didn't make sense to her to have to put all her furniture in storage if I could just keep it in my house until she got back. I agreed since I had a lot of vacant space anyway. She bought he furniture down there, and I was glad. The beautiful velvet maroon living room set and large fish tank brightened up the place.

The first month after she was deployed was good. Then she started calling collect. She said it was because they had messed up her pay when she got transferred and that it didn't get straightened out. She said she would be back home in a month and she would take care of the phone bill. By the time the end of the month came, I had a $700 phone bill. She called and said she would be home the following week and she would take care of it. While she was talking, I heard some female talking in the background. The very next statement was "Come on, baby, let's go." I could have thrown that phone out the window.

"Baby? Really? Who is that? And is that why you all of a sudden been calling collect? You spending your money on someone else?" I was angry all over again. Why did I keep getting involved with all these lying females?

"It ain't what you thinking. She just playing. We talk like that," Carrie said as if I were a straight dummy. I had already been warned about her from a mutual friend who knew her long before I did. I had made a lot of friends when I was with Bev, so there was plenty that was no longer new to me. I wasn't the same gullible person I was with Tammy, and the first sign of a cheat was always the right sign.

"Well, keep talking to her. Even when you come home. I am not your fool or anybody else's. You just told me that you were tired and was going to lie down. You are going to lie down, all right, but not by yourself." I wasn't buying it.

"There you go, talking all stupid. You know what. I am done with this. I will be home next week, and I will get my stuff out of your house!"

"You will not get one piece of furniture out of this house until you pay that $700 phone bill," I told her.

"You can't hold my stuff hostage! It's mine, and I am coming to get it," she said.

"Try me," I said, and I hung up the phone. I knew she wouldn't call back, because she had already showed her true self and I wasn't on her mind at all.

That next day, I called her commanding officer. She must not know whom she was dealing with. I explained to him that one of his soldiers owed me for a phone bill and I expected her to pay. He told me he did not and could not get into social matters but since she was a sergeant, he would have a private discussion with her.

The next phone call I got from her wasn't collect or civil. She was livid that I called her commanding officer and put him in her business. She called me everything except my government name and told me she was coming to get her furniture and there wasn't anything I could do about it, and she hung up the phone. Well, she didn't have a key, so I didn't know how she planned on getting it.

The following week, the plan unfolded. My principal called me outside my classroom, and he wasn't very nice.

"Ms. Ross, you're a good teacher, and I like you, but your personal business is not to be a part of school grounds," he started off saying, and I was confused by him even talking to me since I knew he didn't know. "There is a young lady in the office with the sheriff stating that you have some property that belongs to her and she will press charges if it is not returned. I don't care to know, and I don't want to know, but I suggest you handle this matter very quickly before it gets any worse." Then he walked off.

I could have spit fire right there in that hallway. I went to the office, and there she was with the ugliest smirk on her now-ugly face. She was lucky we were on school grounds and she had the sheriff there with her; if not, we would have been rolling right that very minute.

"Sheriff, I am at work, and I soon as I get off, I will allow her to get her stuff."

"All right, make sure it happens," he said, and he walked off with her trailing behind.

The nerve of that lying, cheating, useless body coming to my job. Now my principal knew, and it would only be a matter of time before the rumors started floating around. The next few hours didn't go fast enough. I left work and went straight home. She was there waiting along with the sheriff. Well, she ain't all that dumb after all. I opened the door and stood off to the side. I asked out loud while she was wrestling with that heavy furniture about the phone bill, and she just sucked her teeth and said, "What phone bill?"

Yeah, she is dumb, but I won't allow her the satisfaction of seeing me beg her for anything. I just stood back and enjoyed her wrestling with that furniture by herself. Neither I nor the sheriff wasn't interested in lending a hand. After she loaded it all up, I slammed my door. There I was once again. Alone.

I was in a weird way for the next few days—angry, hurt, confused, relieved, sad, and trying to avoid the looks my mother was giving me. She wasn't too happy how everything had gone, and she said some of her worst fears were coming true, that I was getting deeper and more involved with the wrong people.

That weekend, I headed back to where I knew best—the club in Savannah. On the way there, less than fifteen minutes from home, I saw a familiar sofa beside the highway, all busted up. It looked like Carrie didn't know how to load or tie down a load. I laughed so hard I almost ran off the road. I felt relieved and justified just seeing that sofa mangled up beside the road, imagining the look on her face when it happened. I guessed that was my $700 paid in full.

I spent the next few months back and forth to Savannah on the weekends. I had quite a few one-night stands and nothing beyond that. Most of the time, I would be leaving Savannah on Monday mornings fully dressed to go to work. I would get to school and be dog-tired and hungover from a weekend of partying. That went on until someone local caught my attention. We dated for a while until my mother got wind of it and she hit the roof. She said that if I were going to carry on like that, I didn't need to do it around there.

I could lose my job. I could lose everything. The town was too small, and everybody knew everybody's business. It hurt to hide, and it hurt even more to break up with her. I really did love her a lot. But my mother had a point.

I was back on the prowl again at the club.

One-night stands and drunken Mondays became the routine. My drinking had increased a lot, so much to the point that even during the week, I would take a sip. On one of my excursions to the club, I met my next obstacle. Her name was Maria; she was beautiful. She was 5'11 and taller than me. She had a beautiful smile and a butt to match. When she talked, she had a northern accent that made my ears fall in love. We talked, we danced, and we went back to my hotel room, and six months later, we were alternating times of travel. She would come down and see me, and I would go up and see her. She was stationed on base in Savannah, and she confessed to me being her first as well. I enjoyed our time together, and we travelled a lot on the weekends and when I was on break. We even drove up to her hometown in Baltimore for Thanksgiving, and I met her mom. I remember going to the club in DC, and I was blown away. The club took up the whole block practically, and it was packed. I was falling deep, and I didn't want to get up. I didn't want it to go away. We partied together a lot—house parties, clubs, block parties, private parties—if they had them we were there. My circle of associates and friends began to widen even more as we both would meet people and exchange numbers to be invited to the next get-together.

One weekend, she came to visit, and as usual, we went over to my mom's to eat. My had a strict rule about washing your hands before coming into her kitchen. Maria spoke, and they chatted a minute. And then she went straight to the stove, picking up the lid off the pot

"Hey, go wash your hands befo' you go in my pots," my mom said.

Maria raised her hands up and said, "My hands are clean. I washed them earlier." She laughed, holding up her hands as supposed proof.

"I don't care. You just walked outside and 'cross the yard, and you need to wash them again before you go in my pots," my mom told her.

Maria slammed the lid back down on the pot and turned toward my mother. "I said I already washed them. Don't worry about it. I don't want anything to eat anyway." And she stormed out the door.

My mother looked at me, and she didn't have to say anything. I was just as mad as she was.

"I know, Momma. I got it. I will handle it," I said as I stood there a minute and collected myself, and then I left as well.

Walking back across the yard to my house, I was furious. She had just been rude to my mother. The last time she was here, she had flirted with my daddy. Of course, I was the only one who knew she had, but this act of indignation just took the cake. I had never been disrespectful to my mother, and I wasn't going to allow some other female to be rude to her either. When I got into the house, Maria was sitting on the sofa with a drink in one hand and a cigarette in the other. At that very moment, she was no longer attractive to me. I wanted to slap that cigarette out of her hand and throw the drink in her face and bring her a dose of reality. I decided not to take the physical route because my mother was next door and who knew what would have happened. I propped up against the wall and just stared at her. She kept her eyes glued at the drink in her hand and kept taking drags on the cigarette—long deep inhales and slow exhales. She finally finished the cigarette and dabbed it out in the ashtray. She didn't say a word until the bottom of the glass was empty.

"Say what you gotta say, and be done with it. I am really not in the mood for a conversation," she said as she grabbed the bottle off the table to pour another drink—all straight, no mixer. As much as she could drink, I didn't see why she even bothered to pour it in a glass. She should have just taken it straight from the bottle. I guessed that was her way of being a "cute" drunkard. Yeah, in her mind, it was cute. In my mind, it was a problem.

"I really don't appreciate your tone or your attitude toward my mother. Her rules are her rules, and we as well as anybody we bring into her house has to abide by her rules. Your slamming that lid and not doing as she asked was one thing, but for you to raise your voice and get an attitude with her, that will not be tolerated from you or anybody else." I tried to remain calm and spoke very slowly so she would understand every word that I said. "Not only that, you will go and apologize to her."

"Apologize? For what? I don't see anything I need to apologize for! She started with me!" she shot back and then downed the rest of the drink.

"Once again—and I need you to understand this is not a request—your tone was unacceptable. Your slamming the lid and not abiding by her rules was unacceptable. Your raising your voice was totally unacceptable, and your attitude *stinks*!" I said as I counted each offense on my fingers in front of her almost-drunken face. She looked at me, and then she stood up. Yes, she was taller than me, but she couldn't fight a lick. I knew it, and she knew I didn't have a problem picking her big butt up and throwing her across my shoulder. I had already shown her I wasn't a pushover. So her standing up and getting in my face didn't threaten me one bit or change my mind.

"And if I don't apologize?" she asked me.

"Don't drink no more because you will be driving back to Savannah in about five minutes," I said, meaning every word.

"Really? Are you serious? You're gonna put me out? I just got here, and you're gonna make me drive back all because you *think* I had an attitude with your mother? Are you really?" She was mad, and her words showed the beginning of her drunkenness.

I didn't say a word. I just stared at her. Part of me was hoping she wouldn't apologize. I could just be done with her and her drunkenness. Yes, I was a drinker as well, but she doubled my intake. She stood there looking at me as if I would change my mind and join her in the drinking party, but I was not in the mood. She stomped her feet like three-year-old having a tantrum and twisted back and forth.

"All right, all right! I will apologize, but only because you are making me."

"Just make sure it's not with an attitude, and we will be okay. If you go over there with an attitude again…" I didn't need to finish the sentence. She understood I wasn't playing.

"All right, all right," she said, and then she stomped out the door.

I wasn't going with her. If she didn't do right, my phone would be ringing before she made it back. I sat down and turned on the stereo. I knew the apology wouldn't change how I was now feeling about her. At least, it would ease the tension for my mother, but I knew that things between her and my mother as well as the relationship that we had would never be the same. When she came back a short time later, she was actually laughing. I guessed that meant that things went well. That was good but just a little too late. There was already a deep wound, and the bleeding had not stopped with her laughter. I survived the weekend, and when she left, I prepared myself for the inevitable.

The bomb finally dropped a few weeks later after I didn't go visit her and she didn't come visit me. She called one afternoon and said that was confused about us and didn't know if she could continue the relationship. He ex-fiancé had returned from oversees, and he wanted to see if they could work things out. She talked, and I listened. Whatever she said, I wasn't going to try to change her mind. I was fine with her decision and told her to call me if she ever changed her mind and needed someone to talk to, and she said she would. I hung up the phone, knowing that would be the last time I ever talked to her. The silence after I hung up the phone was a echo of a position I had been in too often. I was alone, no real friends, just names of folks I knew written in my gray phone book. I didn't know whom to call, and I didn't want to talk to anyone. My own mother was next door, and as much I as wanted to talk, I couldn't make myself walk a hundred feet to go talk to her. I was not going back to the club this weekend. I had enough of the one-night stands and the club relationships. I wanted something more meaningful, something that would last beyond six weeks or six months. I was drowning in broken relationships and alcohol. I lit a cigarette and puffed, realizing my life and my relationships were just like this cigarette—good when it was first lit but a short time later was over and had to be put out, only to have to light another one to try to get that feeling of that very first one. That feeling never came, but the addiction had already taken root and could not be overcome. My body wanted more, and the more I smoked, the more I wanted. It was the same with the women. The more I had, the more I wanted.

X6

Summer 1992

Her name was Paula. I met her through a mutual acquaintance, and she was beautiful with a very infectious laugh. She had the prettiest white teeth that spread across her face when she smiled. When she would put on a pair of Daisy Duke shorts, they would scream for mercy. Our initial conversations and meetings were rather friendly. She was still strung out over her ex-girlfriend and not interested in a relationship. I poured on the charm. I refused to be outdone by a past cast member. Any and everything she wanted, I did, or I bought it. Eventually, the charm took its effect, and after months of wooing, she gave in. We were just like two schoolgirls giggling and laughing all the time. Shortly afterward, the town became too small for me and my lifestyle. Paula had persuaded me to apply for other schools in larger areas to get me out of the country. My mother was in agreement. She said I needed to move to where nobody knew me and start all over.

t the festival and only
e awarded the superior
unty Middle School
from Taylor County
were awarded the

ty Middle School's
ie" and it was about a
ot being accepted.
eighth grader at
rt of Artie and he was
ctor" trophy for his

tstanding
by Stone, Sumter
l's Ashley Hancock,
rochu, and Karen
d job as members

at Sumter County
d the One-Act play

I applied to several schools and eventually was hired and relocated to Sumter County. It wasn't the country with dirt roads, and it wasn't a large metropolitan area either, but it was a move that was much needed. I found an apartment, and Paula eventually moved in as well. Two months after moving in, she called me on the job and told me we had to move. She had just witnessed a rat run and leap into the trash can and jump back out with a chicken bone. I wanted to just die laughing on that phone. Here she was, a nurse, around the sick and the dying, and scared of a rat.

Nevertheless, I obliged, and we found a better apartment on the other side of town. It was rather nice, and the days and the months flew by. No one knew us, and since we were in a town with a college, we always told everyone that we were roommates, and no one bothered to investigate further. Life was wonderful, and we made friends in town and expanded our circle out of town.

Paula became bored with the nursing home and applied to a program that was about an hour drive away; the pay was better, and she would be working less hours. I agreed knowing that our time together would increase because she would be working less days. That went quite well for a while, and then our time started dwindling. Sometimes she wouldn't come back. She would stay with her cousin in Macon. I was fine with that and insisted she had a cell phone installed in her car since she was traveling up and down the road quite a bit. That helped our communication gap quite a lot.

I had a friend who was more like a sister and relationship that I had never had. She made me smile and laugh, and I would do anything for her. I couldn't remember in the time that we had been together where we had ever argued or had a disagreement. I had found that relationship that I been looking for, and I was happy. When Paula would come home, we would travel to Savannah, Jacksonville, Atlanta, and other places and hang out and party. Then the trips started getting fewer and fewer. There were times it would be weeks at a time before I would see her.

I went to the mail and checked the box one day, and there were the usual bills. I opened the cell phone bill, and I was beyond belief. $1,200. I went through page after page after page, not recognizing any of the numbers, and very few of them were the house phone. I went straight to the phone and tried to call her. No answer. I called her job number, and apparently, she had quit over two weeks ago. I was dumbfounded. After almost two years of being involved with Paula, I was wondering if I even knew how to get in touch with anybody to get in touch with her. I didn't. I would have to wait it out. I continued calling the car phone, hoping she would pick up. The minutes turned into days, and finally she answered.

"Heyyyyyy!" she answered as if we had been talking to each other every day. "What's going on with you? And before you say anything—I miss you!" She rushed out her mouth before I could get anything out.

"Well, there's a lot going on, and you would know if you call me instead of all these other numbers on this $1,200 phone bill!" I spit out.

"What? Oh no, that can't be true! I barely even use this phone."

"Well, somebody has, and somebody needs to help pay it," I said. "And while we are talking about pay, when were you going to tell me you quit your job? I called there looking for you, and they said you quit over two weeks ago."

"Why would you call there looking for me? I don't need everyone in my business. Besides, I have another job," she said, sounding irritated.

"Well, I don't have any other numbers to call, and since when is it an issue for me to call you? It's not like you have been calling me! Is there something you need to tell me? Is there someone else?" I asked with very little patience.

"I really don't have time for this right now. I will be back there in a few days, and we can talk about it then. But no, there is no one else. I have a lot going on right now, and I really don't have time to answer a million questions. We can talk about it when I get there," she said and hung up the phone.

I sat there with my mouth open, ready to say, "Hold on just one minute!" But there was no one listening but the dial tone on the house phone. I felt very stupid at that moment, an unexplainable kind of stupid, like I was staring in a mirror "looking at myself and not even recognizing my own face" kinda stupid. Something was not right, and whatever it was, I didn't even know where to begin as to what it might even be, so I would just have to wait and see.

When Paula finally showed up that Friday, she wasn't alone. She had some guy with her that she introduced as her cousin James. They came in, and I was waiting for an explanation that never came. She took a shower and changed clothes, and I felt as if I were the punch line in a big joke. After changing clothes, she tried to reassure me that everything was fine and that there was nothing to worry about, that we were as solid as ever. She said she just needed to see me and reassure me that we were okay and that there was a lot of work that had her caught up, and that was it. She told me to just relax and everything would be fine. When she smiled that big pearly white smile, I was convinced, and the uneasiness went away. I went to the store to get some beer and wine coolers, and we all sat around, talking and laughing. Her cousin was pretty cool and crazy as well. It started getting late, and he said he had to work tomorrow. She said she would drive back since he had drank more than any of us. I said we could both go, but she said no, that she would be going back to Macon as well for work. I hesitated but agreed and knew I had to be to work Monday as well, so that wasn't going to work.

I stood at the door and waved them both goodbye and felt better than I had felt in weeks. She called throughout the weekend, and we talked and laughed as usual. By Monday morning, I was back to my usual pleasant self. Shortly after lunch, I got called to the office for an urgent phone call. I picked up the phone, and it was my bank. They were calling to inform that I had a lot of unusual activity on my debit card. They read off the list of transactions, and I didn't recognize any of them. There had been over $650 worth of withdrawals from different banks within a two-day span. She asked me if I had possession of my bank card and if I didn't, who did? I told her I thought I did, and she wanted to know if I approved the withdrawals. I told her that my card might have been stolen, I wasn't sure, and I wouldn't know until I got home and checked since I didn't carry it on me. She said that they could put a hold on the funds for up to forty-eight hours but that I would need to let them know so they could press charges if the charges were unauthorized. When I hung up the phone, I wanted to scream. The secretary asked me if everything was okay, and I said I would be okay and walked out of the office and back to my classroom. I couldn't escape the madness in my head or the possibility of what could have happened. I kept retracing my steps and seeing where there could have been a miss or an opportunity for me to misplace my card. But she said there were withdrawals and the only way there could have been withdrawals was if someone knew my PIN. Oh, hell, nah. I just knew this heifer didn't do that. Paula was the only person that knew my PIN other than me.

As soon as the buses loaded, I left school and went home. I checked the drawer where I kept my card, and sure enough, it was gone. I didn't care what the reason was. Nothing was going to be good enough. I was just waiting on the phone to ring. Paula had been calling at exactly 5:00 p.m. every day since she left. The next forty-five minutes lasted forever. When the phone rang, I didn't even have a chance to say hello before I heard her frantic voice.

"Listen, I need help. I am in some serious trouble, and I need help!" she jabbered.

"Well, whatever trouble you are in, it just got worse. You took my ATM card, and you took money out of my account. If that money is not deposited back with forty-eight hours, the bank is going to allow me to press charges. They said they would hold the funds for forty-eight hours, and after that, it's up to me as to what happens next."

"Baby, please, please don't press charges. I can get the money back. I just needed it to take care of something, and I was going to get it back to you. I promise." Her words sounded as desperate as she did.

"Oh, so now I'm baby? You took money from me, my rent money at that, without any regard as to what was going to happen to me, and now you want me to look out for you? You have forty-eight hours!" I said and hung up the phone. I didn't want any explanations, excuses, or sad stories. I wanted my money back. The only way the bank would not take it was if I pressed charges and filed a case of theft. I never got any more calls that day or the next. When Wednesday rolled around, and I didn't get that 5:00 p.m. phone call, I knew what I was going to have to do first thing Thursday morning.

I lay across the bed and started crying. I was embarrassed, hurt, mad, confused, and lost. What started as a great relationship and friendship was now a complete nightmare. I must have fallen asleep because when I heard the banging on the door and looked at the clock, it was 2:00 a.m. I looked out the window, and there was Paula. The only thing I could say to myself was, *She better have my money!* I opened the door, and she rushed in like she was being chased.

"I know you're mad. I am so, so sorry. I just needed to take care of something, and I didn't know how to ask. But I got your money, all except $150, but I have a stereo system in the car, brand new, never been opened. You can get the money from that to make up the rest. Just please don't press charges," she said in between breaths. She sounded exhausted, and she looked strange. I was trying to remember what she was supposed to look like, but I really didn't know this person that was standing in front of me.

"What the hell am I going to do with a stereo system? Is it hot? If it is worth so much money, why didn't you sell it and just give me the money?" I asked her as she started pacing back and forth.

"Look! That's all that I have! Take it or leave it!" she hissed at me.

I stood there and put my hand out for the money, and then I counted it to be sure—$500 dollars in every denomination there was, mostly $1 bills. I had nothing to say to her. I took the money and stuck it in my bra.

"Where is my card?" I asked with my hand out again. "Never mind. Don't even worry about. The bank already froze that one. I will get another one. Good night," I said and headed toward the back.

"I said I was sorry. Please don't make me go. I don't have any-where else to go. I lost my other job. My cousin is nowhere to be found. You are all that I have right now. I know I messed up. Can I please stay? Most of my clothes are still here, and my mail still comes here. I just need somewhere to sleep. Please." She had already started crying before she said please.

"You can stay, but you're sleeping on the sofa." I went into the bedroom and locked the door behind me. I made sure all my valu-ables were relocated, and tonight would be the first night I slept in a bra, with the money pinned to it with a safety pin, like my mother used to do. I was mad, and as foolish as it may sound, I loved her.

When I got home from work the next day, there was dinner waiting for me. It was weird at first, but after we started talking and she began to tell me everything that had been happening, I started relaxing. She reminded me of the person I had fallen in love with and not the stranger that had popped up on my doorstep. I had worked everything out with the bank, and I just took the hit on the $150. We never made any agreement or reached a conclusion on the $1,200 phone bill. That was another loss I would have to take since the phone was in my name.

The next couple of weeks went about the same. I went to work, she stayed at home and cooked and cleaned, and we would laugh and talk when I got home. She still had the sofa. I wasn't giving in that much. She said she had been looking for a job but hadn't had much luck. I told her not to give up so soon, that something would turn up.

I didn't know how long that cycle went on with us as room-mates, but it actually felt a little better than being in a relationship. One day, I was at work and she came right after school had let out and said she needed to get my truck. She said that she was going to help a friend move some furniture and that they were going to pay her. So she gave me the keys to the car and left in my truck. I asked if she needed help, and she said no, that I should go on home and she would see me when she got home.

9:00 p.m., no Paula.

12:00 a.m., no Paula.

3:45 a.m., no Paula.

6:47 a.m., no Paula.

6:55 a.m., a knock on the door.

When I opened it, there was a police officer at my door. He asked me for an ID and asked if I was the owner of a black-and-grey 1991 Chevy S10.

"Yes, I am, Officer. Is there a problem?" I asked, nervous about what his response was going to be.

"Ma'am, I am going to need you to come with us to the station for some questions," he said.

"Before I go anywhere, can you tell me what this is about? Am I under arrest?" I said, backing up slightly.

"No, ma'am, but we need you for questioning regarding the trafficking of marijuana," he stated.

My head started spinning, and my heart started pounding. I didn't even smoke marijuana. How in the devil was I supposed to trafficking it? "I need to call my job before I go with you and at least let them know I will be late."

He said, "Go ahead."

I picked up the phone and called my best friend who worked at the school to let her know what was happening. I told her I would explain everything later but that I was headed to the police station for questioning.

When we got to the police station, I felt like I was in a TV show. This was not real. This was really not happening. They took me into the office area and sat me in a metal chair. An older guy in a suit and tie came in and sat down in another chair backward and scooted up toward me. He mumbled a couple of words about the right to remain silent and some other garbage and asked me if I understood. I told him no, that I didn't understand. I didn't understand why I was there. I didn't know what they wanted or anything else.

He asked me what was my relationship with Paula Smith, and I said, "We are currently roommates. Yes, we used to be in a relationship, but we are now just roommates." He asked me how long I had known her, and I said almost four years. He then asked me why she was in my vehicle. I told him that she had asked to borrow it to help a friend move some furniture and that I had let her borrow it. He asked me whom I knew that stayed in some trailer park on the north side of town, and I said I didn't know anybody up there. He asked me if I was sure. I told him yes.

"Sir, I don't know what is going on or why I am in here. Can you please tell me what I am in here answering all these questions for?"

"Well, we arrested your friend Paula for possession of marijuana with intent to distribute. We have been watching her for a while now, her and a couple others. So we saw that she had switched vehicles, and when we stopped and pulled her over, she had in possession fourteen ounces of marijuana, and there was a loaded gun under the seat. Do you know anything about any of that? Be honest, because right now you are in the hot seat," he said and leaned in close enough for me to smell his stale breath.

"No, sir, I don't know anything about any of that except the gun. The gun is mine. My mom gave it to me for protection when I am on the road by myself. I don't know nothing else about no marijuana or no trailer park or none of that. I let her hold my truck to move furniture. I didn't know all of that was going on." I was getting agitated. What fresh hell was this that I had been drawn into?

He left, and I sat there motionless for about an hour. I wanted to cry but not in front of them. As the time on the clock crawled by, another guy in a suit came in and said they had all that they needed and I would be given a ride back home. I asked about my truck and if I could get it, and he said no, that it was being impounded. I asked for how long, and he said until they finished the case. I asked about the gun, and he said I should be thankful that they didn't charge me for an unlicensed gun. I just looked at him and walked away. He must have thought I was dumb.

You can't charge me with that anyway. I wasn't driving the vehicle.

I got back home and wanted to just scream. It was a good thing they kept that gun because if I had it, I would shot the first person that knocked on my door. I was just that mad. The phone rang, and it was Sandra, my best friend. She said she was worried, and when I explained to her everything that had happened, she said she couldn't believe it but she would do some digging around to see what she could find out. She knew everybody, and it wouldn't take her long to get all the dirt. She told me I would need to call my principal and let her know what was going on before the "street committee" got to her.

I was dreading that phone call more than calling my parents. I would have to call them, especially since my vehicle was impounded. I called the principal, explained everything as best as I could, and reassured her that I had nothing to do with any of that. She said she believed me but that my association with it did not look to good for me. She said she would see me when I got to work. She said staying home was not an option.

I was glad I listened. Being at work was a welcome relief and a distraction. Unfortunately, that distractive state came to a halt after I made it home. I received a collect call from the jail, and it was Paula. I accepted the charges only because I really needed to hear what she had to say. She was already crying when I said hello.

"Ugh, I...am...soo...sorry..." she said between sobs. "I never meant for any of this to happen, and I don't even know what happened."

"Start from the top—from the point you came and got my truck," I said.

"I went to Marty's, and we had already made a couple of trips and moved some furniture and a lot of stuff. On the third trip, we got pulled over. The police said someone had reported a stolen trampoline and that they had seen the truck in the area. So they asked us to step out of the vehicle. They searched it and boom! They found your gun under the seat, and apparently, Marty had a bag of weed, which I didn't know about."

"Ummm, it wasn't just a bag. It was almost a pound. Nobody smokes that much!" I said, getting angry.

"I promise you, I promise you, I didn't know! I was just doing a favor for a friend, and look what happened. I was just trying to make a couple of dollars, and look what happened. I didn't know he had that on him. So since I was driving and it was a loaded gun in the vehicle—unregistered—I am now in here. I don't know what I am going to do. I can't stay in here. Can you please help get me out of here? Please, I didn't do anything." She was begging, and I had never heard her beg for anything. She usually just told me what she wanted, and *bam*, I made it happen. At whatever the cost, I made it happen. This was a whole different kind of making it happen.

I contacted Sandra, and she gave me the scoop on everything. Apparently, Paula was hanging out in the trailer park regularly while I was at work. She had began to affiliate herself with a couple of folks that were on the police's radar. So the stop that night really wasn't for her but the passenger. That still didn't help her case much with the law. They weren't gonna allow her bail, so she was stuck there until her court date. I didn't know how I felt at that exact moment. I didn't know if I was relieved or saddened. It was a whole mix of emotions. That was the beginning of sorrows.

There were a couple of certified letters that had come in the mail addressed to Paula. When I finally got a chance to talk to her, she told me I could open them to see what the letters were about. The first was the same as the next one. She had checks that had bounced, and they were allowing her to come pick them up before they pressed charges. So of course, she talked me into picking them up and paying the fines so that she wouldn't have anything on her record. It wasn't just one or two. Over the course of the next few weeks, there were about ten of them. I told her I was exhausting all my funds and I couldn't keep it up. I had found someone who was willing to help her with her case so she could get out and handle her own mess.

I was at the point where I really didn't care, but I would help her get out, even though I had been told by several folks to let that go and let her drown in her own vomit. I couldn't turn my back. She was my friend. Here I was worried about her, and my world was falling apart. My truck was still impounded, and they weren't going to release it. The word had gotten around at my job, so of course, folks were looking at me strangely. There were more and more envelopes coming with "Certified" on the outside and threatening letters inside. I was slowly drowning.

Paula finally got a court date, but she still wasn't going to be released, not without a large bail, and I couldn't afford it. I was sent to the pastor of a local church by one of my coworkers. She said he was an advocate for folks who were first-time offenders. When I went into his office, he had the biggest smile on his face, and I felt the weight being lifted just walking into his office.

"So I hear you have a small problem," he said, still smiling.

Small was an understatement. *Small* was a long way from where I was currently residing. As a matter of fact, the only thing that was small at that present time was my bank account.

"Well, I guess that's one way of looking at it."

"So tell me what we can do to help," he said and leaned forward to get an ear full.

I didn't know who the "we" was, but if "they" could help, it wouldn't matter. So I told him everything from the beginning, and he listened and never once interrupted me and asked any questions. When I finished, he leaned back in the chair and closed his eyes. He sat there in silence, and I could hear the clock ticking on the wall. I didn't know how long he stayed that way, but I was glad when he finally opened his eyes. I thought I had given him a stroke with all that I said.

"Well, give me your number, and I will give you a call later after I check out a few things," he said and smiled. There was something about his smile that made me feel safe and protected. I didn't know whether to shake his hand or take a bow. I decided not to do either one. I gave him my number and told him thanks and went home. I didn't know whether to laugh or cry. I didn't even know why I was doing anything to help. I just knew that seeing her cry and looking so lost did something to my stomach and made me want to stop the tears. She reminded me of a lost little child that needed someone to point them in the right direction.

I didn't hear anything back from the pastor that night, and that made me return to hopelessness. I muddled my way through the next day in a zombie-like state, waiting on the next blow. After work, I went straight home, fell across the bed, and the wall finally fell. I cried and screamed and cussed at the walls. Of course, the walls didn't care either. I fell asleep and was awakened by the phone ringing.

"Hello," I said, sounding like a drunk.

"Well, are you ready to come pick up your friend?" the voice said and then started laughing. Through the phone, I could see that safe and protective smile.

"Are you serious? How? When? Is this for real?" I asked without stopping.

"Yes. Meet me down at my office at the church, and we will go from there."

I hung up the phone without a goodbye or waiting to see if he said anything else. I went to the bathroom to wash my face, and when I looked in the mirror, I looked a mess. My eyes were puffy and swollen from crying. My hair was all over the place. I stared at myself and didn't like what I saw or whom I had become. Someone else was controlling my every move and my every thought like a puppet on string. Today I was an ugly puppet. I quickly turned away and shook my head, hoping that would shake away my thoughts. I was not gonna let my looks spoil the moment. My friend was getting out of jail after being in there over a month. By the time I got to the pastor's office, Paula was already sitting in his office. I didn't know whether to hug her or punch her in her face. A whole mixture of feelings started swimming in head, and I could only stare at her. She looked wounded and sad. Those pearly white teeth were now hidden behind a sad face and a head hanging on slumped shoulders.

"I am sorry for all this. I really do appreciate everything that you have done to help me get out. And, Reverend Stone, I really want to thank you for getting me out. I don't know how I can ever repay you."

"I know how you can repay me." He paused, and his smile was no longer there. "Show up for court," he said with firmness, and then he smiled. Paula started sobbing uncontrollably, and he got up and put his hand on her shoulder.

"It's going to be okay. We all at some point make bad decisions. We all have at one time or more in our lives trusted the wrong person. The true sign or maturity is learning from it and having a heartfelt desire not to do it again. You will be fine. You both will be fine. Now go and take a hot shower and relax, and you will feel much better." He turned and looked at me and smiled, and there was an assurance in his smile that made me trust everything he said.

The ride back to the apartment was spent in silence. The only noise was from Paula sniffling and sighing. I had never seen her cry this much. I couldn't say anything. I couldn't fuss. I couldn't yell. I could only look straight ahead and try to keep from crying myself. Paula when straight to the bathroom and closed the door when we got home. I sat on the side of the bed, looking at the wall and then my feet. I heard the water and still didn't know how I should be feeling right now. I really didn't want to talk. I was glad she was out but pissed at everything that had happened. Then I felt sorry for her. I couldn't even imagine what it was like to be in jail. I guessed she missed the bathtub because she stayed in it forever. When she finally came out, she looked a little better, and she tried to force a smile, but the tears soon made that go away.

"Don't try to talk about it. Just go lie down, and when you are ready to talk, we can," I said, and I wanted to hug her, but that old stubborn mule in me said, *No, she don't need no hug. She needs her butt kicked!* "You are welcome to the sofa. Right now, that's all I can give you." I clenched my teeth so I wouldn't tremble or cry when I said it.

"I understand. I am glad to at least have that. I love you," she said and walked out the room. I wanted to throw up. Love? If what I was dealing with was love, then love me less *please*!

The next couple of days were more of the silent awkward moments after I got home from work. By day three, I was dreading going home and drove extra slow going home. When I got home, Paula was in a different mood. She actually was smiling and rather talkative. She said she had talk with Pastor Stone and there was a good chance her case might be dismissed. He would let her know when he had finished working on the details. I was somewhat happy as well. The smiling pastor had some connections. I was impressed. She was excited, and it scared me. I felt like I was in the room with Dr. Jekyll and Mrs. Hyde. Her mood change was a shocker. She talked about what happened the day she was arrested and her days in jail, and there were no more tears. It was as if the news had erased all the emotions of what had happened. By the weekend, she was in overdrive. She was excited about her cousin James coming to visit, and I welcomed the company as well.

We sat around laughing and talking, and I grew tired before they did. I decided to go to bed, and she said he would be leaving shortly, so I said good night and went to bed.

I woke up the next morning with a light headache. I don't know if it was stress or that I had finally gotten a good night's sleep. I went to the bathroom and then to the living room. No Paula. I stood frozen for a minute and paused. This was a one-bedroom apartment. There were no other rooms to check. I looked outside. My heart sunk. The car was gone. I stood there with the door wide open, staring at the empty space. I shook my head to shake away the negative thoughts; maybe she just went to the store. Yeah, that was it.

Two hours later, I knew that she wasn't gone to no store. I just knew this heifer didn't leave me in my car. Yes, the car and the truck were in my name. Her credit was shot, and now I could see why. The truck was still in the impound, so I was stranded with no transportation. I sat around the house steaming all day Saturday. I had no way to call. I didn't have any phone numbers for her. Sunday came. No Paula. I hoped she would have the decency to come back before

I had to go to work Monday morning. Sunday night, no Paula. I was madder than a wet hen. Monday morning, no Paula. I called Sandra and asked her for a ride. I was too embarrassed to tell her why, and thankfully, she didn't ask any questions. But I knew that wouldn't last long, especially if I had to ask for a ride the next day. Tuesday morning, no Paula. I was more mad than worried. I called Sandra again for a ride, and I knew there would be questions. When I got in the car and before she could ask, I told her everything that had happened since Paula had gotten out of jail. She was silent for a moment, and then she hit her hand on the steering wheel.

"Look, you're my friend, and I love you like a sister. But you are gonna have to let that go. She don't mean you no good, and the word on the street is that she's on something. I'm not trying to scare you or hurt you, but something ain't right. You need to open your eyes and see it," she said.

I sat there in disbelief, but some things started making sense. Even before she was arrested, I felt something was off. I couldn't put my finger on it, but there was a lot of weird stuff going on. I was blinded by it all. Paula was extremely intelligent, beautiful, and a hard worker. Drugs? I didn't see it in her, but it would explain everything a whole lot, especially now. When I got home from work that day, I needed answers, so I started searching. I did something I had never done before, and that was go through all of Paula's things. I went through her clothes, her bags, her pocket books, shoes, everything. My momma always told me, "If you go looking for something, you will find it. Just be sho' your heart can handle what you find." I now understood what that meant when I opened a small bag and found a small copper tube with foil on one end. On the other end was a short glass tube. The whole thing fit into the palm of my hand. I really didn't know exactly what it was, but the way it was hidden in the pocket of a gym bag rolled up in a paper bag reminded me of the earlier conversation with Sandra. I called her and told her what I had found and asked her if she knew what it might be.

"Girl, that's a crack pipe!" she yelled. "I knew it. These folks in these streets ain't lying." She said that as if that was the final answer. I stood there with that mess in my hand. She had stolen from me, got my truck impounded, lied to me, and now I was stranded for a $10 high.

"I gotta go," I whispered. I knew I couldn't stay on the phone with her. I couldn't let her hear my brokenness. I couldn't let my friend see me fall apart any more than she had already seen. She had a husband and kids. What did she know about the pain I was going through right now? What could she say to me to make me feel better? What could anyone say to me? I didn't know who Paula was anymore. I didn't even know who I was anymore. All this time, I had been fighting to hold on to something that didn't want me. All this time, I was scratching, clawing, and digging to make ends meet and just to have someone suck it away in a pipe. I shook my head in disbelief. This had to be someone else's. She had a lot more sense than that.

She probably didn't have that much sense. Wednesday morning, still no Paula. I was tired of hitching a ride. I was having to hear about this and that. I was walking around in a zombie-like state at work. I didn't know what was going on, and I didn't care. I got home that evening and sat looking at the walls. Somebody knocked on my door, and I walked nervously because no one just showed up around here. It was Sergeant Jackson. He was a recruiter for the army, and we were good friends. He and his wife and kids stayed one row over in the complex, and he said he was just checking in on me since I had backed out of enlisting. He saw my face and asked what was wrong. I told him everything I could tell without crying. I told him I had no way of calling Paula and that I really didn't want to call the police. He told me to give him all the information I knew and he would see what he could find out. He was originally from Macon, and he knew a lot of folks. He really felt like I needed to call the police. I felt real stupid and small. I didn't even know my own license plate. He said he had enough information to go digging around and he would let me know what he would find.

Then I remembered the cell phone bill. Why didn't my dumb butt think of this earlier? I gave him the bill and told him this was the only thing I had with phone numbers. He said that would help a lot, and then he left. The look on his face said enough as he walked out the door, shaking his head. He was worried about me as well.

I sat on the sofa and stared at my empty hands. They reminded me of my life at the moment—empty, cracked, dry, and lifeless. The ringing of the phone startled me. I picked and said hello, only to hear complete silence.

"Hello, hello, hellooo!" I said and was about to hang up.

"Wait, don't hang up, please." It was Paula. "I know you're mad. I know you are upset, but I just couldn't stay there. I had been locked up in jail and then locked up in that house. You were looking at me as if I were guilty, and you didn't want me around. I had to—"

I cut her off before she could finish. "You are selfish and ungrateful. You left me with no transportation, knowing I had to go back and forth to work. You weren't out of jail a week, and you ran off after everything that I did for you and tried help *you*! Now you have the nerve, the unmitigated gall, to say I was looking at you like you were guilty! You *are* guilty—of thinking only about yourself and whatever else you are doing," I spewed.

"No transportation? You can go get your truck," she said as if she had all the answers.

"I *can't*! They won't release it!" I paused to take a deep breath because this wasn't helping. It had been almost four years since I had a cigarette, but I felt that urge starting to burn in my mouth while talking with her.

"Oh, I didn't know. I thought they would after I got out," she said nonchalantly as if we were just shooting the breeze.

"Listen, I really don't have time for all this. I need the car back so I can go to work," I said. "I really don't want to have to call the police, but I will." I was hoping she wouldn't call my bluff. There was silence and then a deep sigh.

"You don't have to do that. I will bring it back," she said, talking through her teeth.

"When?" I was not in the mood for conversation.

"I will be back by the weekend," she said.

"The weekend?" I asked in disbelief.

"Yeah, I should be able to dig up some gas money by then. I have been staying with my cousin, and she is not going to front me any money. Just don't call the police. I will bring the car back," she said.

I didn't know whether to believe that or not, but at this very moment, what choice did I have? I just hung up the phone. I was upset for a minute. Then I hit *69 to see what number she had called from. I was in luck. I had a number finally. I called Sergeant Jackson and gave him the number to see what he could come up with. I felt some relief.

Friday morning didn't start too well. I picked up the phone to call Sandra for a ride, but there was no dial tone. I slammed the phone down. It was off. I hadn't paid the house phone bill. I chuckled to myself. *Hadn't* wasn't the right word. I *couldn't* pay for it. I hoped she would remember to come get me.

After she picked me up, I regretted that as well. She still had a lot of questions, and I really wasn't in a talkative mood. So I listened until my mind floated elsewhere, and I tuned her out. My being at work was no different. My body was there, but that was it. By the time I got back home, I was even more miserable. Now with no phone, I was super isolated. I watched TV as long as I could, and then I decided to walk to the store up the street to use the pay phone. I made a few calls and went inside and sat down in one of the booths. The mother of one of my students was the manager, so she didn't mind at all. She said she welcomed the company. I sat there a while, and then an older white gentleman came into the store. He approached me and asked if he could sit for a minute. I told him sure, and he just started talking about everything. He reminded me of a small version of Santa Claus. He had snow-white hair but no beard. We chatted for almost an hour, and then I said I needed to go. He followed me out the store, and when he saw that I was walking, he offered me a ride. I told him I only stayed a couple of blocks, and he said I shouldn't be walking while it was dark. I agreed and waved goodbye to my student's mother as I got in the car. She waved back and went back to work.

Steve told me quite a bit while we were sitting there. He worked with a construction company that was clearing some land in the area. He had been in town a couple of weeks. He was married but had no kids, and he told me about several of his adventures. While he was driving, he began talking again. We were about to approach the apartment complex, and I told him to slow down.

"Hey, that's my turn right there," I said, pointing toward the complex entrance.

"I know, I know," he said. "I just want to show you where I work. It's not that far. I really want to get to know more about you."

There were no stop signs or traffics lights for him to stop at. The farther away he drove from the complex entrance, the more concerned I became. I could see we were heading to the outskirts of town.

"Would you please just take me back home?" I was afraid. I had seen stuff like this in the movies, and here I was, the starring character. Steve didn't answer. Before I knew it, we were way outside the city limits and turning down a dirt road going back into the woods. We finally came to a stop in the middle of nowhere. There were no lights, no houses, nothing but trees, and we were parked in front of an area that was being cleared for construction. This man was going to rape me and kill me—was all I could think at the moment. He pulled something from his side and placed it on the dashboard. It was so dark I couldn't make out whether it was a gun or what. I wanted to cry. I wanted to scream. It was all Paula's fault.

"All I want is a pretty li'l girl like you I can talk to. When I come to town and work, I can see you, and we can do some things. This is where I work, and I just want to spend time with you. Just me and you," he said as he put his arm on the back of the seat behind me.

It had been a long time since I prayed, and I didn't even remember what to pray. I just whispered to myself, "Please, God, help me."

"Can you please take me back? Ms. Williams knows I am gone, and she knows that I left with you," I said, trying to remain calm.

"Who is Ms. Williams?" he asked.

"She was the cashier at the store. She is one of my students' mom," I said.

"Oh, umm, well, I didn't mean no harm. I just wanted to talk and spend some time with you," he said, moving away from me.

"I want to go back," I said, never looking at him once. My eyes were straight forward, and my heart was saying, *Please, please, please.*

He finally started the car and backed out. I wouldn't breathe a sigh of relief until I was safe inside my apartment. He took me to the complex, but I directed him to someone else's apartment front door.

"Listen, I really didn't mean no harm. I just wanted to have someone I could spend time with and get to know. Can I come in and sit with you some more?" he asked.

This has to be the worst nightmare ever, I thought. There must a "Stupid Girl" sign on my forehead.

"No, I don't think that's a good idea. This is the last conversation. I'm sorry, but no," I said as I was opening the door.

I stood outside the car and walked backward, keeping my eye on him as he started the car and drove away. I made sure he was gone, and then I ran back to my apartment. I rushed inside and locked the door and fell flat on the floor. My stomach was in knots, and I almost peed myself from being so scared. I started hitting myself on the side my head for being so trusting. I hadn't learned a lesson yet about trust. If someone told me something, I believed them with no research, no doubts, or no reservation. Look where it had gotten me—deserted, with no vehicle, in the middle of the woods, with a complete stranger who wanted "a pretty young thang to lay up with," a crack-smoking girlfriend, and no phone to even call the police if this man found out where I stayed and came back. *Unreal!*

I stayed in all day Saturday. I was afraid to even walk outside to go to the mailbox. I was becoming a prisoner now and I didn't like it at all. My insane moment was interrupted by a knock at the door.

"Who is it?" I said with voice in a deep growl, trying to sound like a man.

"Sergeant Jackson. Is Lane home?" he asked, sounding unsure of whom he was talking to. I must have sounded pretty convincing.

"Hold on," I said, still in a growl.

I opened the door, and he looked over my shoulder to see if he could see anyone. I started laughing and told him to come in. I was actually glad to see him.

"I hope I didn't interrupt anything," he said, looking around in the room like someone was going to pop up.

"That was me, crazy. I was making sure it was someone I could let in."

"Who you hiding from?" he asked.

"Long story, and I don't want to repeat that for nobody," I said.

"Okay, I don't even want to know then. On the flip side, I have an address for you. I had to do some digging, but I know where you can find her cousin and her." He plopped the papers on the table.

"Well, that helps a lot, but how am I supposed to get there?" I asked.

"I can give you a ride there—on one condition." He paused and just stared at me.

"I am afraid to ask," I said.

"Only if you promise me we won't be making no blank trip. I don't want you getting there and listening to no sob story and changing your mind. If I take you, you are coming back with just the car and *not her*," he said with an emphasis on the last two words.

"After what I have been through, you really didn't even have to add all that," I said.

"We can leave first thing tomorrow morning. It's too late now. She's probably in the streets."

"Okay, just give me a time because my phone is off." I was embarrassed to even say that.

"I already know that. I have been calling you. That's why I came by. We can leave around 7:00 a.m. That will give us plenty of time," he said, and I knew he meant business.

Shortly after Sergeant Jackson left, I began to wonder if this was going to be necessary. She said she was coming.

You idiot, and you believe her?

I was at war in my own brain. I was torn between belief and utter disgust at the thought of trusting her yet one more time. My mind went back to the crack pipe I found, and I shrugged everything off and decided to go to bed with hopes that tomorrow would hurry up and come.

Sergeant Jackson was on time. I didn't expect anything less; he was in the military. The ride to Macon was only about an hour and a half, but it seemed like forever. Sergeant Jackson told me he had some connections on the police force and from the numbers, I had given him and the description and name of Paula's cousin, he was able to get an address. He made sure he emphasized that this wasn't going to be a blank trip and that he would be forever mad at me if I allowed her to suck me back into her foolishness. I could only agree and nod my head. I felt embarrassed, mad, hurt, used, and lonely, even with him sitting in the car. Once again, I was on my own. This time, however, I was broken. I was financially in a rut and emotionally in a pit.

By the time we arrived at her cousin's house, my stomach starting turning in knots. Sergeant Jackson looked at me like "If you don't get your scary behind out this car…" and didn't stop looking until I had opened the door. I went to the door and knocked. Some woman answered the door and looked at me strangely.

"Can I help you?" she said, placing her hand on her hips.

"I am Lane, a friend of Paula's, and I am looking for her. She said she was staying at her cousin's, and this is one of the numbers that showed up on the phone. I really need to talk to her." I was sounding desperate.

"Well, she ain't here, thank God. I am her cousin Fran. Come on in, and let's see if my husband may know where she is," she said, and she stepped back and motioned for me to come into the house. "James!" she yelled. "Somebody looking for you." Then she turned to me. "He'll be right out. Have a seat. I gotta go to work. I will get all the details later." She waved her hand and walked out the door.

Well, at least I was on the right track. James was here. I knew him, or rather I had met him a couple of times. I hoped he wasn't going to play dumb. James came out in a T-shirt, some sleeper pants, and slides like he had just rolled over out of bed. He looked surprise to see me and tried to wake up some more.

"Hey, what's up, Lane?" he asked.

"I was hoping you could tell me. Paula never came back after you both left from down there, and I need the car. She left me stranded, and I have been hitchhiking a ride all week. She said she was coming back the weekend, but of course, that didn't happen. I only know half of what is going on, and that part ain't good. So if you can tell me where she is, I would appreciate it. I know y'all kin and all, but she has really done a number on me."

"Man, I been telling that girl she need to slow down and go back. She has been on the wild side since she's been here. She been renting that car out and everything. I haven't talked with her in a couple of days, but I know where she been holding up. Listen, if you promise to keep quiet, I'ma call her and let you listen in so you will know what's going on. I am not going to tell you. You will have to hear it for yourself," he said.

I could only agree and hope my anger wouldn't get the best of me, making me blurt out and cuss her out on the phone. James dialed a number and told me to pick up the other phone as it was ringing. Paula answered the phone and sounded like she didn't have a care in the world. He asked her where she had been and why he hadn't seen her, and she went to talking and telling everything. She had "stunted" on a couple of folks and scored a couple of times, and everything was just peachy clean. She was talking as if she had been living the life with no intentions of coming back, like she had promised me.

James could see from the expression on my face that I was about to blow, and he steered the conversation. "Hey, I tell you what, I am about to jump in the shower and run some errands. Where are you gonna be in about an hour? I need to drop something off to you," he told her.

"Well, I was going to go make a drop, but I can meet up with you. I need to go take a bath myself. I tell you what. Meet me at June's house, where I have been staying, and we can go from there. See you in a few," she said and hung up the phone.

"Well, at least you know she's all right and where she is going to be," he said to me. James wrote down something on a piece of paper and told me this was where I could find her.

"You're not going with me?" I asked.

"Nooooo, if I go, she'll know I set her up. Whatever you do, don't let her know you got this from me," he said. I guessed he was half-loyal, if there was such a thing.

"All right, thanks, I will wait about thirty minutes before I show up, but please don't call her and tell her I am coming," I asked.

"Nah, you straight with me. I been trying to get her to do right by you, but she on a whole 'nother level. I hope you can talk some sense into her," he said as he lit a cigarette.

The way he inhaled it and blew the smoke as he talked reminded me of the routine. The smell of the smoke brought the taste to my mouth, and I was about to ask for one but decided against it. I was not going to ruin my four-year cigarette-free self-appointed medal.

"Hey, man, thanks. I really appreciate this. I hope this works," I said and left out the door.

Sergeant Jackson had been sitting in the car the entire time. He was looking at me, waiting for me to spill all the details. I showed him the paper and told him Paula would be at that address. He said it would take about twenty minutes to get there and he hoped she would be there. I agreed and felt a sudden wave of sadness come over me. I had heard everything that was said on the phone and couldn't believe that I had been made a fool of once again. I made sure I had everything in. I was not going to cry in front of Sarge. I refused to let him see that part of me.

When we arrived at the address, I saw the white Nissan Maxima parked in the driveway, so I knew that she was here. This time, Sarge didn't have to look at me. I jumped out of the car as soon as he parked. I went to the door, and I rang the doorbell, hoping she would answer. When the door opened, the look on her face said it all. I just held out my hand and looked at her.

"Give me the keys to the car, and I will be on my way," I said.

She looked over my shoulder and saw Sarge in the car and decided not to argue. She sighed and walked away, leaving the door open. I wasn't going in. I didn't know whose house this was, and I didn't care. She came back and put the keys in my hand.

"You have the keys. Can we please just talk? I need to tell you something, and then you can go. I just need to explain. Please." She started begging.

"What is it that you can possibly say to me right now?" I said to her, trying not to blurt out everything I had heard on the phone.

"Just a few minutes, and then you can take the car and be on your way," she said, sounding tired and exasperated, nothing like the person on the phone earlier.

I walked back to the car and told Sarge I would be a couple of minutes. Why? I didn't know.

"WHAT? For *what*? What could she possibly have to say to you?" He was upset. I had never seen him this way.

"I don't know, but I have the keys, and nothing is changing my mind. I am still coming back by myself and with the car. I promise you that," I said.

He looked at me in disbelief. "I am going back home, and if your are not home an hour after I get home, you don't have to worry about me helping you no more," he said, and he drove off.

I had to get this over with. Sarge and his wife were good friends, and I didn't want to lose them. I didn't have many friends as it was, so the few that I did have were dear to me. I went back to the house, determined to hurry and get this over with so I could get home and work on putting my life back together. Paula told me to come in and have a seat. She looked worn and fragile. Someone came out of the kitchen, and she introduced herself as June, Paula's cousin. She and Fran were sisters. So James was just the in-law.

They both sat down, and Paula took a deep breath. "I don't know how to say this, so there really is only one way to say it," she said and paused long enough for me to look at her for her to spit it out. Her attitude and her whole demeanor was different from it was earlier on the phone.

"I'm pregnant," she said and dropped her head.

Well, one thing I know is, it ain't mine, I thought. It took a minute for the words "I'm pregnant" to sink in on top of everything else I had heard today. *Okay, this is a joke.* So I started laughing. They both looked at me strangely, and their expressions made me realize that this wasn't a joke.

"So what are you gonna do?" I asked and realized I shouldn't have asked. I was being drawn back in, and I didn't want to feel sorry for her. I didn't want to care. I didn't want help. I just wanted to leave.

"I don't know yet. I just don't know," she said before she started crying.

Oh, hell, here we go. I can't go through this again. I can't fall for the okeydoke tears. I needed to stand firm.

120

"You know what? As mad as I am right now, I can't think. I need time to process all this. So I am gonna go, and I will have to call you back. Give me a number to reach you, and I will call when I can. The phone is off, so you can't call me. I don't know what to say about any of this."

She wrote down a number on a scrap of paper and handed it to me. I stood up to go, but before I could reach the door, Paula was on her feet.

"So you just gonna leave me like this?" she asked as if she was shocked.

"No different than the way you left me," I said, and I walked out the door.

Some people were so selfish and inconsiderate. If everything wasn't revolving around them, then they wanted to cry foul. As long as they were giving you their butt to kiss and you were kissing it, they were fine. As soon as you took those lips away, they wanted to look back and wonder where your lips went. Love, peace, and hair grease. Goodbye!

X7

Summer 1996

It had been almost two years since I walked away from Paula. I started back on the cycle of one-night stands and random encounters. I wasn't teaching anymore, so the worry and the stress of trying to remain incognito was over. I had left Americus and moved to Albany to move in with Maranda and her two kids. It was a different type of atmosphere altogether. She worshipped the ground I walked on and treated me like a king. I didn't have to try to win her over. She was won from the very first moment she saw me. Before I moved in, we would talk on the phone for hours. I had finally gotten myself financially straight after Paula and had my own vehicle, and I even had a beeper.

I met a lot of her friends, and it was nice. One of her fiends was a hairstylist, and she would do both of our hair. Whenever I would go to pay, Maranda would tell me not to worry about it, that it was already taken care of. So this was how this was supposed to work. Not all one-sided.

I got off from work one Friday and headed to the beautician to meet Maranda for one of our biweekly appointments. When I got there, Jess, the beautician, said she had some bad news. She said Maranda had been arrested for "boosting" in Winn Dixie.

"What? Boosting? Boosting what?" I asked in straight confusion.

Jess looked at me like I crazy. I didn't know what was going on. She stopped shampooing the lady's head that was in the sink and asked me to step outside. She said I had to promise not to tell anyone what she was about to say. I recalled correctly, being arrested was public information, including the reason for the arrest. I told her I wouldn't say anything. I just didn't tell her for how long. She began to tell me that she and Maranda had a deal. Maranda would boost hair products for her, and in exchange, she would do her hair and, as of lately, mine as well.

Oh well, I guess free for me isn't free after all. When do I get a break from all this drama and foolery? She said that Maranda would call me later and that there was nothing else she could really tell me. *You have already said enough for a lifetime*, I thought to myself.

"I won't. I don't understand all this," I said as I scratched my head.

"Just go home, and she will call you," she said, and she went back inside.

The only thing I could say was "Here I go again with another convict."

First was Paula, and now this one here. The years had mended the ill feelings between Paula and me. She and her new girlfriend had actually hung out a couple of times with me and Maranda. It was as if nothing had ever happened. Now they were happy and giggly, and there I was with the button on repeat. I went straight home. The kids would be home soon afterward from school, and I didn't know how that would go.

Oh my, I am now responsible for two kids. I know them, but I don't "know" them.

Before I could get into the house good, the phone was ringing off the hook. I picked it up, and that familiar recorded voice was the same: "You have a collect call from—an inmate at the Dougherty County Jail. You will be billed—. Do you accept these charges?" This was where I always paused and thought long enough before it asked again.

"Yes, I accept." I did not do so joyfully, but I accepted anyway. I didn't say hello or anything. I just waited for the excuses to come; and just as I figured, they came.

"I am so sorry. I don't know what happened. I promise you. Me and Jess were in the store, and yes, I was boosting a couple of things. But then I saw how this one dude was following me around, and I went and put the stuff back, but by that time, it was too late. The guy was an undercover security guard, and he called the police. Jess had already left me and gone to the car. I promise you, I promise you, I have never done anything like this before. I just got caught up," she said. "You have got to believe me."

Nothing she said matched what Jess had told me earlier. So I wasn't going to believe anything beyond "I am in jail." That was the only thing truthful right now.

"Well, have you talked to anyone about bail?" I asked.

"No, and it's Friday, so I won't know anything until Monday. I just know I don't want to be in here," she said, and then the crying started. Apparently, she didn't know me well enough to know that those things didn't work on me. You could cry a river, and I would wait until you were done so we could start talking sense. I was not moved by crying. I should be the one crying. I was the one here with two kids that ain't mine.

"I guess we will have to wait until Monday. What do you want me to tell the kids when they ask? They are gonna ask, you know," I said nonchalantly.

"I know. Just tell them I am with a patient until Monday. When Monday comes, I should be out of here," she said.

124

Maranda worked at a nursing home, but she had never been gone for two days. I would make the best of it with the kids until then. I told her we could hold off on the phone calls until Monday. I didn't want to take the chance that the kids would pick up the phone and know what was going on.

The weekend went smoother than I expected, and that was a relief. Of course, they asked where there mother was, and I repeated the lie she told me to tell. They didn't ask except for that one time, which was odd, but I didn't pay that any attention until later. The kids left for school Monday morning, and I left for work. Maranda called as soon as I got home, like she had a camera in the house and knew when I walked in the door. I could hear the disappointment in her voice.

"I went before the judge today, and I didn't get bail," she said.

"No bail? For hair grease and shampoo? That's crazy. Did they say why?" I asked, getting confused by the minute.

"No, but they gave me a number to the probation office for me to call and see what they could do," she said.

"What's the number, and whom do I need to talk to? Maybe I can see what's going on. Do you want me to call?" I asked. "I don't know how long I can keep up the charade with the kids." I was desperate.

"Just call the probation office. The number is in the phone book. And ask for Ms. Williams. She probably won't tell you anything, but you can try," she said.

At this point, I had to try something. None of this was making any sense, and I felt like I was being torn on the inside. Of course, I loved her, and I cared about her. I hated that this had happened, especially since I was here with the kids by myself. They didn't know what was going on.

"Call me later if you can. I will try to call," I said and hung up the phone.

I called the number in the phone book and asked for Ms. Williams. I told her who I was and that I was a friend of Maranda Davis. I also told her that I was taking care of her kids until she was released and I was trying to find out when that might be.

"I am sorry, but Ms. Davis has thirty days for probation violation," she said with no pleasantry in her voice whatsoever.

"Thirty days! I am not understanding that for something that's a misdemeanor," I said. I had learned a few things in my dealings with Paula regarding the law and infractions.

"If you want to know anything else, you will have to talk with her. That's my decision, and it will be thirty days. You have a good day," she spit out before she hung up the phone.

Okay, now something don't sound right. How can you get a probation violation if you have never done anything? The little hamster on the wheel in my head went to turning.

I heard the kids come into the house, and the first thing they asked was where their momma was. I pretended not to hear them and told them to go to the kitchen table and do their homework. I went into the bedroom and locked the door. Whatever was going on, I was going to find out. I couldn't deal with any more lies.

I searched in the closet through everything I could find. I checked all the dresser drawers, and then when I got to the nightstand, I hit the jackpot. In the bottom drawer was all her paperwork and everything. I found a thick envelope that had the probation office's address on it. I opened it up, and there was four pages of charges all for the same type of offenses—shoplifting. So this wasn't the first time. This wasn't a misdemeanor in the eyes of the probation office. She had violated her probation, which I didn't even know she was on, and as a result, she had to do the time. I just looked at the papers in total dismay.

How unreal can this get? I should have known something wasn't right. But nooooo, here I am believing everything somebody says regardless of how long I have known them. I trust too easily and take everything at face value and look where it got me—again.

When Maranda called that night, I told her I knew everything there was to know and that there was no way she could tell me anything differently. She broke down and started crying. She asked me if I would stay there with the kids until she got out and not to just walk out. I told her I would. I didn't see any reason why they would have to suffer because of her repeated mistakes. I was more mad than hurt.

I was more mad at myself than I was at her because I was back in another dead-end relationship that I knew wasn't going to last. Once the trust had been destroyed, there was really nothing left but good-bye. Unfortunately, this one would be while coming since I agreed to stay with the kids. That was what they didn't ask too many times where she was. They had been on this merry-go-round before.

I immediately started making preparations by looking for somewhere to live. Maranda would still call, and we would talk, but it was obvious where everything was headed. She told me that when she got home, I didn't have to leave. She said I could move into the spare bedroom and we could be roommates. I agreed, thinking that it wouldn't be a bad idea.

After the thirty days were up and Maranda came home, it was rather tense at first, but that eventually leveled out. We were sleeping in separate bedrooms and laughing and talking outside of that. One night, I went through my phone book and called a few friends that I hadn't talked to in quite a while. Most of the conversations were all about the same and not very lengthy. I called Lisa, and our conversation went a little longer than the others.

Lisa and I had met a house party in Jacksonville sometime ago when I was with Maria. We had exchanged numbers and maybe talked here and there but nothing in depth. We had both graduated from Georgia Southern, but I never knew her when I was there. It wasn't a small school, so it was possible not to know everybody. At the time when I called, she was at a party with a few friends, and she promised she would call me back at the first opportunity. We talked couple of more times after that, and I began to notice that Maranda's attitude toward me starting changing. I heard more doors slamming more often, and the cuss words started getting a little more frequent, but they were never directed toward me.

Okay, it was time to go. Even though she had said we could be roommates, I didn't think that she meant that I could go on with my life. I thought the roommate deal was a way to keep tabs on me. I wasn't about to live like that. I found a place, but I needed help when it was time to go because I could sense the tension and the last thing I wanted was to fight my way out. I called Paula, and she came with her girlfriend. Yes, even after all that she had done, we were still friends of some sort. If I called, she came. If she called, I came. We just weren't going beyond that. I could never go back, and that was my rule. Whenever I left or the other person left, there was no going back. It was a done deal. It became too messy and too much might have transpired in between.

Of course, I was right in calling for back-up. Maranda was pissed. She tried to remain civil in front of Paula and Michelle, but she was chewing that gum like a thoroughbred horse chewed hay. She kept her hands folded on her chest, and she would only stop chewing long enough to make snide remarks and to say how low down dirty I was for walking out. She said she hoped that whomever I was whispering to on the phone at night would make me happy. She was going on and on about me using her. Really? I was here with your kids while you were in jail for thirty days, and I used you?

I packed everything I could get in my silver box Chevy, and I couldn't pack it fast enough. I didn't have any furniture; I just had my clothes, shoes, pictures, and a few other things I had collected. Whatever wouldn't fit in the car would just be left behind. I wasn't going back to get anything. I gave her back her house key and walked away. I was relieved and ready to move forward and into my own place.

I had found a mobile home for rent in a trailer park away from Maranda. I didn't tell her where I was going, and she didn't ask. It wasn't the best, but it was peaceful and just me. I was happy to be in my own spot. Lisa and I had been talking regularly, and we had even made plans for me to visit her. She stayed about two hours away in a small town where she was a teacher and a basketball coach. She had recently gone through a breakup with her girlfriend, and she was in the same spot I was in—recovery. We both weren't ready to rush into anything because the wounds were still raw and oozing from our past relationships.

Lisa was different from anyone else that I had ever been involved with previously. She was mature, classy, independent, and very goal oriented. She probably had her daily schedule written down on index cards so she wouldn't miss a beat. She was meticulous about her appearance, her hair, her house, and her job. I didn't pay it much attention when she first said it, but I did when I went to visit her.

"I am glad you finally made it to see me," she said as she opened the door with her big gorgeous smile.

"I have been looking forward to this for a while. I just needed to make sure I had worked through all those other issues before I involved anybody else."

"I am glad you did, because I don't need any of that coming this way. I do have my job to think about, and I don't want anyone in my business. I hope you can understand and respect that," she said. The beautiful smile was already gone, and there was a very serious look on her face.

"I may need you to explain what you mean. It sounds as if you think I am going to write a letter to the newspaper about you," I said, starting laughing.

"I am not joking. I have a reputation to uphold, and I am not about to tell this one or that one. I don't even want my parents to know," she said.

Okay, now I am understanding. I can really understand that part. I wish sometimes I could go back in time and redo all that again myself, especially since the person who put me out there decided to have some hidden secrets of her own and dump me in the process.

"Well, you don't have to worry about me saying anything. I already know what it is like to be put on blast. I do understand, and I respect that," I said, knowing the last thing I wanted was to have any drama from anywhere.

The rest of that weekend was quite magical. We sat and talked and laughed and relaxed. It was truly a different experience for me, and I welcomed the relief. Of course, time always flew when you were having fun, and the weekend quickly came to a end. Leaving was quite painful, but I knew this would be the scenario going forth and that it would be for the best.

I was met the next day at work by a beautiful bouquet of flowers, the first of many that would come to my desk. They were the talk of the office, and so was I. Every female in there wanted to know what guy was so thoughtful. I laughed every time they asked. They didn't know, and I wasn't telling them. There was only one person whom I had shared that information with at this office, and that was Grandma. That wasn't her real name, but that was what I called her. She was a lot older, in her late forties, and she didn't gossip like all these other fresh-outta-college folks. She reminded me a lot of my mother, except for her South Carolacky accent. Not only were we coworkers, but she and her family lived in the same trailer park that I did. I had told her about Lisa, and of course, she gave me the same lecture my mom gave me. She still said she loved me no less and said she would keep praying for me. I thanked her and made it through the rest of the day smiling and dodging jealous eyes.

The next few months were wonderful. I had weekend excursions all over with Lisa. I remember getting back to work one week and not feeling that great. Whatever it was, I hoped it would pass before the weekend. I didn't want to miss out on another great time. By that Wednesday, I was miserable. I went home from work, and I was nauseous. I thought maybe the hotdogs I had for lunch were doing a number on me. I tried to vomit and couldn't. Then my stomach started cramping severely, and I was getting lightheaded. I went to the store and got a bottle of Pepto-Bismol and returned home. I read the label and it said not to take it with the symptoms I was experiencing. I thought if I lay in the bed, the pain would go away. The bed only seemed to make it worse. I called Grandma and told her I was going to the emergency room and that I would call her when I got back.

After I arrived, they immediately started running tests. The did a urinalysis, an equilibrium test. They checked my ears, nose, and throat. They did an X-ray, and after the X-ray, they had to give me a barf bag. I was dry heaving, and only bile was coming up. The doctor finally came back and said I had a stomach virus. They would give me something for the nausea and send me back home. I made it back home, and the medication they gave me made me groggy, but the pain only got worse. I couldn't even make it to the bed, so I lay across the sofa, and everything went dark. I was in an out of consciousness all night. I felt my bladder about to burst, and I tried to get up but couldn't move. I could only roll over onto the floor and crawl to the bathroom. I was in so much pain. The next time I opened my eyes, I was on the bathroom floor, so I crawled back to the sofa. When I opened my eyes again, the sun was glaring through the window, and somebody was banging on my front door.

"Who is it?" I could barely open my mouth; it was too painful.

"It's Grandma! Open the door!" She sounded impatient. I tried to sit up, but my body would not cooperate again. I rolled off the sofa and crawled to the door and could only reach up and unlock it.

"My god, child, what ails you? You can't walk?" She was shocked.

"I don't know. My stomach hurts too bad. They said last night at the emergency room that I had a stomach virus, but this ain't no virus," I whispered.

"Well, come on, I'ma take ya to my doctor," she said, trying to help me off the floor. She sat me back down on the sofa and picked up my phone and made a few calls. She called our job to let them know what was going on. She called her husband to tell him where she was going, and then she called her doctor's office. She explained to them what was going on, and they told her to bring me in immediately.

With her assistance, I was able to make it to her car. The drive to the doctor's was short, or maybe it was because I was in and out of consciousness again. We went inside, and they took me on to the back rather quickly. They asked me to relive all the last few days, and I explained as best I could everything that had taken place and what they said when they released me from the emergency room. I told them about all the tests they had taken, and the doctor asked if they did any blood work. I told her no. They drew blood, and it wasn't long before they came back and said that my white blood cell count was extremely high; I also had an elevated temperature, and my overall appearance was frightening. The doctor said she was calling the hospital and that I was to report to the emergency inpatient area. The doctor said that my condition was critical, but she didn't say what the diagnosis was.

We left and went to straight to the hospital. They took me to the back, and Grandma was right by my side the entire time, until they sent me for some more X-rays. It wasn't long after the X-rays that I was lying on a hospital bed. Two doctors came in. I knew something was really wrong because this was the fastest I had ever gotten to see a doctor. They introduced themselves as internal organ surgeons and began to explain.

"We are going to have to perform surgery on you. Your appendix is the problem. There seems to be some other things going on, and we won't know for sure until we get it removed. So we are going to get you prepped for emergency surgery," he said. They asked a couple more questions, and then they both left.

I looked at Grandma, and she squeezed my hand. Her look of worry must have come from mine. I gave her my mother's phone number and Lisa's number and asked her to call them and let them know what was going on. They led her out of the room and rolled me out to another room. It wasn't long before everything went blank.

When my eyes opened again, I was shivering. There was a mask on my face, and my vision was blurry. I tried to move, but that was not an option. I didn't know where I was, and the room was completely white. I turned to my left and knew I wasn't in heaven because my ex Paula was standing there, looking at me and smiling. She was dressed in her nurse's uniform. I tried to talk, but nothing would come out.

"Don't try to talk. You just came out of surgery, and you are in recovery. I told them I was your sister, and they let me in here. You had everyone scared for a minute. Your mom called me and told me what had happened. I told her I would come and check on you and see what was going on. I can't stay long, but I will be back," she said with tears forming in her eyes.

Oh really, she cares after all that foolishness? Okay, now is not the time.

I could talk, and my body was still shivering. I felt a huge pulling in my abdomen area. I was under a thin blanket with something that looked like a heat lamp over me. Paula walked out, and then one of the doctors came in.

"Well, young lady, we have you all patched up. You probably won't remember much of this, but I need to explain to you everything that has happened. Your incision is very large. Your appendix had actually died, and gangrene had set in. So we had to open up your abdominal area and make sure we cleaned everything out. We are pretty sure we have taken care of everything, but you will be in here with us a couple of days. We will keep an eye you," he said it all very quickly. He then tapped me on my hand and walked out.

When I opened my eyes again, I was in a room with another patient. She was an older lady, maybe in her sixties. She introduced herself and started telling me everything that had happened to me last night. I didn't even know until she told me that it was the next day. The doctor came in and explained again everything he had said yesterday. He said I was lucky that it had been caught in time. A few hours more, and he wouldn't have been having this conversation with me. There was gangrene all over the lower portion of my abdomen, but he reassured me they had gotten all of it out.

I doubted that from the amount of pain that I was feeling in my stomach.

"I am hurting pretty bad," I said, and I still couldn't move or sit up.

"We will get you something for pain, and I will be back again to check on you." He nodded at the nurse, tapped me on my hand, and walked out.

I must be a pet to him, the way he keeps tapping on my hand. I didn't need tapping. I needed this pain to be gone from my stomach. The nurse came back and gave me something for the pain, and she said it wouldn't take long. She was right.

I was awakened by someone pulling the covers up over me. When my eyes focused, I saw Lisa standing there, looking at me.

"You really scared me. Grandma called me and told me what was going on, but I was headed to a game. I couldn't concentrate on coaching or what I was doing the whole while. I am glad you are okay. I came as soon as I could," she said.

It was okay. Whatever the reason, she was here now with flowers in hand, so I was relieved.

Unfortunately, before I could open my mouth, the door opened, and there was Paula. She came in and spoke to Lisa and began asking me how I was doing and if I needed anything. I felt the tension on my left from Lisa. She knew all about Paula and everything that I had been through, and it didn't sit well with her. They were cordial to each other, but that was all for show on Lisa's behalf because she didn't want drama. I told her I was good and that I was having some pain but that they were taking good care of me. She began to talk and explain everything again that she had already told me last night, and I knew that was irritating Paula.

I thought to myself, *Well, Lisa, my momma can't call you because she doesn't know about you because you don't want nobody in your business.*

I saw that Paula was intentionally saying things to irritate her. Yes, Paula knew about Lisa, and she didn't care about her secretive life. I began to squirm a little but couldn't move much. It was if the lower portion of my body wasn't mine and wasn't listening to my brain.

The next thing I knew, there was another knock at the door and in walked Maranda in her scrubs. Wow, this had to be a trick—two of my exes and my current girl in the same room at the same time. I knew full well that none of them cared for each other like that. Yes, Paula and Maranda were cool with each other, but that was it. I went to reach for the cup of water to sip, and before Lisa could get to it, Paula grabbed it and put it to my mouth. Maranda then began straightening up my covers and fluffing up my pillow. I was getting a lot of attention, but it was coming from the wrong ones. I could see the hurt on Lisa's face, and she just blew.

"She don't need y'all help. I got this!" She grabbed the pillow from Maranda's hand and began placing it behind my back. I saw Maranda roll her eyes at Lisa, and Lisa gave her a smirk as well. That was when I heard a machine beeping rapidly.

A nurse immediately came into the room to check to see what was the problem. She looked at the machine, checked my pulse, and told me I needed to calm down. She looked at all them and said very politely, "I am going to have to ask all of you to leave." I could feel my head spinning and my whole body getting very warm.

"All right, young lady, I need you to breathe in and out very slowly and deeply. You have been through a major surgery, and the last thing you need is for your blood pressure to go up any higher than it already is now," she said. "I need you to breathe and breathe deeply." She stood there holding my wrist, checking my pulse, and watching me while I inhaled and exhaled. She checked the machine some more and looked me in my eyes. "I don't know who those people are to you, but if they care anything about you, they wouldn't do anything to upset you right now. You have enough going on, and if they are going to cause your blood pressure to rise like that, then they may not need to come back," she said, sounding like my mother. She checked my pulse again and stayed there until it was better. Then she walked out.

"Baby," my hospital mate said, "I ain't trying to get in your business, but them last two that came in here don't mean you no good. You were just fine until them two came in starting a mess. I was watchin', and I saw what they was doing. They was doing it on purpose," she said and kept mumbling something.

"Yeah" was all I could say. I knew she was right. I didn't know her, and she didn't know me. She was an outsider looking in, and in less that fifteen minutes, she summed up my entire relationship with those two. I felt bad, physically and emotionally. I wondered what effect this would have on my relationship with Lisa and if this would be a problem. I really couldn't think about too much because this dull pain in my abdomen wouldn't go away.

The next day (I could keep up with the days now), Grandma came to visit. She told me she had been praying for me. On the day of my surgery, she had arrived at the hospital. It was getting late, and when my sister showed up and said she would be there for me, she had left. I told her that wasn't my sister and explained who she really was, and she just shook her head. I told her about Lisa and what happened with those other two bandits. She continued shaking her head. She visited for a while, and then she said she had to go home to cook. She squeezed my hand again and left out the door.

When the nurse came in that night, I asked her how long I was going to be in the hospital. She said that all depended on me, that I wouldn't be released until I was able to get out of bed and walk on my own. Walk? My legs wouldn't even move while I was lying still.

I couldn't stay in here. I was miserable and alone. I had visitors here and there and phone calls, but it wasn't the same.

I spent four more days in the hospital. I still wasn't free though. I had thirty-two staples from below my navel to the middle of my pelvic area. So walking was still a challenge. I could get around but not like how I used to. My mom and dad were there to pick my up from the hospital, and my mom insisted I come home with them until my staples were removed. That would be another two weeks. Ugh, as much as I dreaded that, I knew it was for the best. I told Lisa where I was a going and gave her my mom's home number and address. I was headed back to the country. She said she would bring me back for my doctor's appointment. I was glad to see her, but I knew the days would be extremely long in the woods away from everyone. The good news, though, was that if nothing else, my mom would make sure I ate.

When we got to my mom's, I was relieved. I thought I would feel bad, but I felt better than I realized. There was always someone there and always something going on. Unlike at my place, where I was the only voice and body that was there. My niece met us at the door, and she was happy to see all of us. She was only about seven years old, but she was very sensitive. When I made it to the couch to lie down, she came over and looked at me with very sad eyes.

"Auntie, what's wrong?" she asked, almost in tears, as if she could feel my pain.

"I had surgery, so I am little tired and sore," I said, lying backward in very slow motion.

"Where? Can I see?" she asked as if her looking at it would ease her mind. I pulled up my shirt and lowered the top of my joggers, and she started laughing.

"Ooooh, Auntie, you have a zipper on your stomach!" She kept giggling.

I laughed with her and saw that her seeing it made her feel better and made me laugh. I needed that.

Those two weeks flew by quicker than I realized. Soon I was headed back to Albany to get the staples removed and put this all behind me. It was a near-death experience that I wanted to forget. Most of the events were foggy, anyway, as if it were all a dream. The constant reminder, "the zipper on my stomach," told me every day that it was not a dream. Even after the staples were removed, I had a permanent scar that wouldn't let me forget. Thankfully, though, Lisa had forgotten or had at least put the incident in the hospital room with Maranda and Paula behind her. She said she wasn't gonna stoop to their level. She knew her place with me, so she was fine. They were just sore losers, according to her. I laughed. Yeah, I was in the right place with the right one.

The months soon rolled into a year, and the long distance was beginning to wear us both. Lisa finally made the decision to move after a long deliberation and many painstaking discussions. I really thought my frequent visits there were starting to look suspect. She was still adamant about being so private. It was a very small town where she lived. Everybody knew everybody and their business. I knew once she came to Albany, that paranoia would calm down. So I was extremely shocked when she told me she would be getting her own apartment. She said she still needed to keep her life private. I didn't argue with her.

After about two months, she gave in. I could move into the apartment with her, under certain conditions:

1. All my belongings had to go in the other bedroom, and that bedroom had to be set up as if I actually lived in there—in the event her parents came to town.
2. When her parents did come to town, I had to sleep in that room, even though they wouldn't spend the night there. They would get a hotel room.
3. If anybody ever came over, we were just roommates, unless it was our closest friends and their girlfriends.
4. Everyone that came over had to take the same vow: what went on in that apartment and whoever was there—all that—stayed in that apartment.

I figured it would be all right. Other than the one I had with Paula, this relationship had lasted the longest and had the least bit of turmoil and drama.

Our stay in the apartment lasted over a year. Then the constant changing of neighbors and the neighbors' inquisitiveness began to be a problem. I had changed jobs in November of 1998 and was making three times the amount of money I was making when I was working at DFCS. We discussed moving, but Lisa said renting was out of the option. If she was going to be spending that kind of money, she would rather buy. So we looked at houses, and when we saw one that we liked, we went to the bank for the loan. Sad to say, as we sat in front of the loan officer, she had to be the one applying without me. I had filed bankruptcy back in 1996 after everything I had gone through with Paula. I was left with all the financial baggage, and then I stopped working momentarily, so it went haywire with that. The loan officer said once I got my credit straightened, I could be added. My income could count as supplemental income for Lisa, but I wouldn't be on the loan. I was fine with that. Two months later, we had moved into a brand-new house. It was a new house, but the same rules still applied from the apartment. It wasn't too much longer after we moved in that Paula and her issues showed up again.

I got a call from Paula's cousin that he was concerned about Paula and Ezekiel. Ezekiel was Paula's son who was born when we were roommates; we had not been in a relationship but were strictly roommates. I was Ezekiel's godmother. I was there when he came out the womb, and I bonded with him quickly, especially since his mother was distant and didn't know anything about babies. Having eight siblings, I knew about babies. He was over a year old when I moved to Albany, but he was still a part of my life. As a result, when anything happened with her, somebody called me. I called Paula's house. She had moved about an hour away into her grandmother's house after she died. She never answered. I called her aunt who lived across the street and asked if she had seen her, and she said no, that there was no car in the yard. She said that Paula had brought Ezekiel over the day before and that she didn't have any clothes for him or anything. I told her I would come and get him. Lisa didn't argue or try to convince me otherwise. She said he could come stay with us, but she wanted no part of Paula. I understood. I could only imagine what had happened on the drive there. Of course, this wasn't anything knew for me in dealing with her, so I wasn't shocked.

I went to her grandmother's house, and there was no car in the yard. I parked and walked to her aunt's house, and she said Ezekiel was sleeping. I told her I was going to see if I could get in the house to get him some clothes. I knew where she kept the spare key. I asked her to keep him over there until I came back. I didn't know what I would find.

I found the spare key in the shed where Paula had previously told me she kept it. I knocked before I went in, and there was no answer. I called her name when I walked inside, and there was still no answer. The house was a mess. There were ashtrays with cigarette butts running out of them. I walked to the back of the house and toward the side door. When I made it to the den area, I saw her lying on the floor, facedown, in her own vomit with her eyes wide open. I just stood there looking. Then I saw her back rise; she was still breathing. I wasn't in shock. I didn't cry. I didn't rush to touch her. I just stood there in total disgust and anger. I saw about ten pieces of paper on the table with her handwriting all over them. They were goodbye notes to Ezekiel, Cantrell (her girlfriend), and me—in that order. I read each one of them and stuffed them in my pocket. I stood there a little longer, and there was a knock at the door. It was her cousin Melvin. He looked shocked and immediately rolled her over.

"She's still alive," I said with mixed feelings about that. When she was on her back, I could see she had been in that position for a long time. Her arm was frozen stuck to her body and wouldn't move, and she had urine all over her. Melvin was patting her face to try to wake her, and I went to find the phone to call 911. The ambulance came, and of course, they asked a thousand questions. I didn't want Ezekiel to have to go through that or be taken away, so I never said anything about the notes. I told them I got a call from her cousin and I came in and found her like this. I went and gathered Ezekiel's clothes and shoes and found any papers that I would need to get him in school in Albany. He was in pre-K, so it wouldn't be that hard. I followed the ambulance to the hospital. The doctor said she would be in there while. She had done some damage to her body. I wasn't sad or hurt. I was mad. Ezekiel was a bright, cute, and good kid. He should never have to go through the torture his mother was taking him through. As many times as I had asked, she would never give me custody of him. Maybe this incident would change her mind.

It was now a third member in the household, but Lisa didn't mind. She would often go get her nephew and bring him over so they could play together. We were a fun little unit. I did, however, notice that the house rules didn't let up, and they were starting to increase. Our venturing out on weekends had already ceased before Ezekiel came to stay, and there were very few, if any, friends that could come over. We went to the mall one weekend. We were walking along, and she looked ahead of us, at the people coming toward us, and said, "Oh God, that's one of my students!" She immediately turned around and walked to the other side of the mall as if she weren't walking with us. That crushed me for some reason. I had seen her paranoia show up before, but for her to walk away from me and pretend like she didn't know me was unreal. I saw her walking really fast on the other side of the mall, and then she ducked in one of the stores. When I passed by her student, I just spoke and kept on moving. Lisa was nowhere to be found. I stood there with Ezekiel for a minute and felt abandoned, just like he had been. His mother was in the hospital and in recovery, but she had some other things she needed to work through as well, and she knew it. I stood there looking at him, hoping that he would never know that feeling that was wrenching through my gut at that very moment. When Lisa finally caught back up with us, I was not in the mood for any conversation. The only thing I could say was "Let's go!"

When we got home, it didn't feel like our home. It felt like hers—her rules, her regulations, her car. She had a spare key to my car, but I couldn't have one to hers? Her paranoia, her control! We had been in this for almost four years, and it was not changing. I didn't want to talk about it, and she knew I was in a foul mood. I did what I thought was reasonable and calm. I wrote her a letter and explained how I felt since my talking hadn't changed anything. I told her that I was tired of being treated like a contagion when her family, students, or coworkers came around. She would be all kissy-face when it was just me and her. But outside these four walls of *hers*, I was a roommate, someone who paid half the bills and her car note on a brand-new car—and I couldn't even drive it. The last time I drove it and stayed gone longer than she thought I should, she came looking for me. That was the last time I drove it. She said I could, but I didn't want to if I had to got through all that. I was putting my efforts, my emotions, my finances into something that I had no say so in. I spilled everything and asked if there was possibility of anything changing.

I gave her the note the next day before I left for work. When I came home that night, she was drinking. I was used to that by now. It had become an everyday thing. I would occasionally drink as well, but when I did, I didn't know how to stop. The hangovers would make me back off and wait awhile though.

She shook the letter in my face. "You could've just told me this," she said. "We've been together almost four years, and you couldn't just talk to me and tell me how you felt."

"I have been talking to you and telling you, but you don't seem to understand that it's getting to the point now where I am tired of it. Do you see any of those things on that letter changing? Do you see any of your behavior changing?" I asked, hoping she would at least understand my point.

"No," she said. "You knew from the start how I felt and what I expected. I don't see that changing anytime soon. I have my career, my school, my family to think about. I am a principal at a high school now. What? Do I look like jeopardizing all that because you want to be out there and you don't care about folks being all in your business."

The words she threw at me cut me in two. I didn't realize I was the only one with "business." I *thought* I was in a relationship, and it was "our business." I guess because I was no longer teaching, and I worked in a manufacturing environment. I didn't actually have a career. I just had a *job*—a job that was paying half the bills in the house where I had no say so.

"So if nothing's gonna change, then why are we doing this? Why are you wasting your time doing something that you really don't want to be doing, Lisa? Why am I here?" I asked.

She took another sip out of her glass and sat it on the counter. "You tell me," she said and walked off.

I now understand what my good friend and coworker David meant when he said I was being used. Yes, it all was appealing. It was nice, new, and shiny. However, at the end of the day, it was hers and her decisions. I had no input in the matter, not even how the relationship should go. I was pretty sure her parents weren't dumb; they knew. They were educators; of course, they knew. That was an excuse. I was never treated any differently by them, but there was always that feeling of uneasiness because it was always a charade when they came around. Why and how did I keep ending up in the same place—alone, with just the clothes in my closet and some pictures in a box that I would go through when I got to the next place and rip up and throw away? I knew it was over. It was just a formality of how long the arrangement would last. I had been in this spot before, so it was almost a numb feeling for me. It didn't matter how much

I cared, loved, gave, sacrificed, catered to, and/or tolerated; I always drew the short straw.

I stood there looking around, realizing how out of place I had been. When I had my own place, even as shabby as it was, it was mine. I said who could and couldn't come into the door, and there was never a time that anyone was turned away. All were welcome. There was really nothing else to be said. We both knew it. I think she was more ready for it than I was. The days after that, our conversations were all just formality. Until I found somewhere to stay for me and Ezekiel, I could stay on the other side of the house. The only thing that was shared was the kitchen. I think if Ezekiel hadn't been there, I would have been put out on the streets.

As time passed, she seemed rather pleased at the distance between the two of us. She had called us just roommates for so long that that was what I became. No matter how many hot nights and days we had shared together in bed, I was a roommate in her mind. Now that we were living that out, it didn't seem to bother her. That pissed me off even more. I went and cut off almost all of my hair. She just looked at me and shook her head. She told me, "You have really lost your mind now." I couldn't have agreed with her more. I lost that "do girl" mentality and was becoming more sure of myself and what I wanted to do—without anyone's permission. I was feeling myself. I understood what it meant to be my own boss and not have to answer to anyone. I went out a couple of times by myself, as I always did when I went out in Albany. Lisa said she wouldn't be caught dead in a club around here. Whenever we did go out to a club, it was two to four hours away always, and she would be on the lookout for any-body she knew. Eventually, she stopped going to the clubs with me and would do a house party here and there, but she had to know who was going to be there. Oh well, I didn't have that problem anymore, and it felt like a weight was lifted from my shoulders.

I went out this one particular night and saw one of my cowork-ers there with a group of her fiends. I was surprised to see her there. I didn't even know she was in the life. She introduced me to her friends, and there was one young lady that was staring at me the whole time. I bought her a drink, and we talked the rest of the night. They were all down visiting Marsha from Atlanta. They just came out to get out of the house, but they were all just sitting there like they were scared. Regina didn't seem bothered at all. She was all focused on me, and it felt rather good to have someone paying attention to me and not looking around to see who was coming in or walking past the table. She was rather attractive and very well enunciated. Okay, so there had to be a hang-up somewhere. She was too attractive to be sin-gle. As the night progressed, we laughed and talked, and then it was time to leave. They were leaving together, and I offered to give her a ride back to the hotel. We sat outside of the hotel and talked, and I explained my current situation and how that was going. She said she understood. She had just broken up with her girl, which happened to be the first female she had been with.

Okay, now I got the picture; she was green and perhaps inde-cisive. She said that her ex had cheated on her, and she wasn't going to deal with that at all from anybody. I also understood that. I had been in many relationships, and I didn't care how bad they got; I never cheated. My philosophy was that I would always leave before I would cheat. What was the point in getting portions elsewhere? I wanted the whole thing, not a portion. Plus, it got messy from what I had seen my friends go through. Folks got attached and would then create drama. Nah, I had enough drama in my relationship. I didn't need the extra!

We agreed we wanted to get to know each other better, but neither of us were ready for anything physical. I respected her a lot for that. Most of the women that had I dealt with would have been trying to get me into the bedroom with them regardless of how vulnerable we both were at the time. For the next couple of weeks, we talked regularly. Regina was easy to talk to and wasn't very demanding. The phone rang early one morning, and Lisa answered the phone. I heard Lisa ask who was calling, and I saw a frown on her face.

Well, here it goes.

She handed me the phone, and I walked out of the living room and into my bedroom and closed the door. Regina apologized for calling so early; she missed me, she said. I found it flattering, but I knew she was just testing to see if everything I had been saying was true. My conversation with her didn't change, and neither did my tone, so I guessed she had her answer. We talked for a while, and then she said she had to get ready for work. I walked out of the bedroom and was met with the an angry face and angry words.

"Don't have your hos calling my house!" Lisa said, and she went into her room and slammed the door.

Okay, it was time to go. So it was the same thing she did when I was in the house with Maranda. She now had a problem with it when it was someone else. That merry-go-round came back to the same spot really quick. I had to come up with another plan.

My plan was to be out of the house in thirty days. That was the plan. That Friday, Marsha invited me to go to Atlanta and hang out with her, Regina, and a few others for the weekend since we didn't have to work. I agreed after she told me that she would have someone watch Ezekiel. It would be a cookout anyway, so there wouldn't be much watching needed. I agreed and looked forward to it. That Saturday, I packed up some stuff for the weekend, and as I was leaving, Lisa came out the room. I told her we would be back sometime Sunday. She asked me if we were going to my mom's, and I said no and walked out the door. About an hour later, as we were rolling on I-75, my cell started ringing, and it was Lisa. She was fussing and saying everything that came to mind. The last thing that I remember was her saying that when I got back on Sunday, all of my stuff would be sitting beside the road.

So she was going to put me out. It was not just me but Ezekiel as well—we would be in the streets. I drove on until I found the next exit. Then I turned around. I told him we would be going back but we were still going to take our trip to Atlanta. He had a sad look on his face, but I knew he would be okay. I called Martha and told her what had happened and asked if she knew anywhere we could stay temporarily. She said no but that she would be checking around for me. She was livid about what was happening as well. I then called Regina and told her as well. She told me to be careful and to make sure I didn't get into any altercations. I told her that I was fine. I knew Lisa thought more of her reputation and that she wasn't going to do anything crazy. The next phone call was to my best friend, David. I told him what was going on and asked if he knew of any place I could camp temporarily. He told me not to worry, that he and his wife would make a few calls and get back with me. By the time we made it to the house, I was boiling hot. I knew I had to remain civil since Ezekiel was there to see everything.

I walked in through the kitchen and into the living room. On the living room sofa sat a pile of my clothes out of my closet. Lisa came out of the room with a smirk on her face.

"Oh, so you changed your mind?" she asked as if she had won.

"For a minute. I came to make sure you weren't putting my stuff out on the streets. On the way back, it came to me, and I wanted to look you in the face when I told you—if you put my stuff out on the streets, I am calling the police. My name may not be on the note, but the mail that I get at the address says I reside here. I know the last thing you want is for everyone to be up in your business like that. But I promise you, if you put one sock or shoe on the street, I am calling the cops."

"Really?" she asked as if something sounded unreal about what I said.

"Try me and see. You were the one who said nothing's gonna change with us. You were the one who put all the rules and regulations in place. You were the one who moved on as well with all your smiling and giggling on the phone. Oh, but I didn't say anything to you because that's what *you* wanted. The minute I do the same thing, it's a problem. I can't deal with that. You don't like drama? I can't tell. What's all this?" I was about to start yelling, and then I remembered Ezekiel was in the other room.

What I said must have hit home. I could see the tears began to form. *Oh, now you want to cry?* I thought. *All this time, you have not shed one tear that I have seen, but now that there's something going outside of you, you want to cry? I am not moved by tears. They are more aggravating than anything else.*

I walked outside to smoke a cigarette (rule number 5: no smoking in the house). I called Martha and asked if she had heard anything. She said she hadn't. I told her that I was going to have to get my stuff out the house but that I didn't know where I was going. While I was talking to her, David called and I clicked over to talk to him. He said his wife's aunt had a place that I could get but that it wouldn't be completely ready until next week. If I needed it, I could put my stuff in there until the electricity was turned on and they got it ready. I told him that was good. He told me about the deposit and the rent, and I said I was good. I wasn't going to be paying any bills in this house, so yeah, I was real good. I hung up the phone with him and called Martha back and told her I wasn't going this time but that I would catch the next trip. I was going to start packing my stuff and moving it. If I had to, I would get a hotel for the next few nights. She said she understood, but she really didn't, and I wasn't in the mood to explain. I had been down this road before; I knew the drill. I went and found some boxes and came back and started in my room. I would get to Ezekiel's when I finished. As I was packing, Lisa came to the door.

"You really don't have to do this. I was mad and upset. Y'all can stay. I just don't want you to go. I didn't know what else to do," she said, the hurt coming through her voice.

"I don't want to have to leave, but I can't stay here any longer. I don't want to wait for the next time you get mad and then I'd have nowhere to go. I have made other arrangements. If you really mean that, then give me until the end of the week, and I will be gone. You have made it very clear that this is your house. I'm just the room-mate, remember?" I turned back around and continued packing. I heard her walk away, and then a door slammed close.

Friday, please hurry.

X8

◆◆◆◆◆◆◆

Spring 2001

I was working more now, and I had to let my mom get Ezekiel. I no longer had an in-house babysitter when I was working nights, so at the time, she was the best option. His mother was in and out of whatever and hadn't quite gotten stable. My days or nights off here and there were spent on the prowl, and I was having a *ball*! I was released from the jail of that last relationship and was happy and loving the single life. Two of my closest friends, Cantrell and Macy, were always part of the activities. Macy was my number one road dog.

Whatever happened, she was ready—ready to ride, ready to fight, ready to drink, ready to party. Cantrell was Paula's ex. They had been together since I left, and she was totally heartbroken by all the stuff Paula had taken her through. I felt *all* of her pain. We all made a vow to each other that we were not getting serious with anybody, that we were just gonna ride, party, and play with the ladies.

After about a year or more, the bachelor life got rather dull. I missed the constant companionship. Of course, Cantrell and Macy had found partners, and they were both getting serious. I found another companion that would keep my company. I started smoking weed. At first, it was a joint or two here and there, and then one of the "temps" introduced me to a blunt. A temp was someone whom I would kick it with here and there, but I didn't see any relationship value in it. They were just something to pass time with, just like I was to them—no feelings, just fun. I began to balance my time between work, play, and the club. The club scene became my second home. If I had to put them in order of time spent the most, it would be work, club, home. Sometimes home consisted of whom I had met at the club. I was a "performer" and entertainer in the club. I would be the ladies' fantasies while I was onstage and collecting dollars and phone numbers while I was up there.

After one of my shows, an older female came up to me and asked for my number. I looked at her and wondered if she knew who I was. She said, "Yes, I am talking to you. Give me your number." Now one thing I did not do was give out my phone number. I would take theirs, and if I felt like calling them, I would. Her accent gave her away. She wasn't from around here, so no, she didn't know me. She just liked what she saw, and there was something that piqued my interest. She was nice-looking and had nice hair, and even in the dark in the club, she had a beautiful smile. She later told me that she was Puerto Rican.

I guess there's a first time for everything. I told her, "I don't make a habit of giving out my number, but if you would give me yours, I promised I will call." She gave me her number and walked off. I watched her as she walked off. *Okay, maybe I will call.*

I never did call her. When I stepped in the club again, she let me know I didn't keep my word. I apologized and said I was busy. I really had been. I told her I still had the number in the pile with the others and that I was going to call her. I could see her watching me the entire night. I thought it was cute. I did finally call her, and we talked. She could actually carry a good conversation. We spent a lot of time talking. It was most of my free time, to be exact, that was spent on the phone with her. It was refreshing but, at the same time, rather weird. She was the oldest person I had talked to in all my life. She was in her fifties, and I was thirty-three. That was as a huge jump, but I was getting burned out club-hopping so much. I must have been high and drunk when I first met her because I did not see a fifty-year-old woman. I did have a lower age limit, no one under twenty-five, not for a relationship anyway.

The age difference wasn't an issue for her or for me. We laughed, we talked, and we spent time together, and it wasn't a rush and jump-into-bed thing. I thought this might work out very well. I still kept my place, even though I spent a great deal of time in hers. I wasn't ready for that move again. When I moved, it would be something permanent. I was already in the process of having my own house built when I met Monique. The building seemed to drag on, and our relationship was growing. She suggested that I could move in with her temporarily until the house was finished; that way, I could save money for when the house was finished. I was fine with that proposal.

Our living situation was going quite well. Then came the phone call from Ezekiel's school. I was listed as a point of contact, and they were concerned about his appearance and the work that he had not been doing. They had tried to reach his mother, but they hadn't heard from her. I didn't have to guess. Paula had gotten out of rehab and went and stayed with my mother, where Ezekiel had been staying, since she didn't have anywhere to stay. That didn't last too long. My dad told her one night she came back from one of her binges that he had raised nine children and not one of them had been in his house and used drugs and she wasn't going to do that there either. She had to go. She told them both that if she left, Ezekiel was going too. I guessed she eventually saw I was the only one that accepted the packaged deal with her and Ezekiel. She had made her way back to her grandmother's abandoned house to live, where I had found her in her vomit. I explained everything to Monique. She had already heard about the history, and she said that she understood and that I needed to go check on him. She had three kids herself. Two of them were grown and out of the house, and one teenager was living with us. I left wondering what I would find this time.

Not much had changed. The house was in need of some repairs. Ezekiel was happy to see me, and I now understood what the teachers meant. His hair hadn't been cut in weeks, and his clothes needed washing and didn't match. He told me he had dressed himself and he was proud of it. He told me he had a dog and he loved it. My heart broke for him. He didn't know what was going on; the dog that he had was there more than likely to keep his mind off not having all the other things that kids normally have. He was six years old now, and he was still a happy child in spite of everything his mother had done. She would call me every time she got in a crunch, but she wouldn't let me keep him permanently. I asked him where was his mother was, and he said he didn't know. She told him she would be back later and to stay with the lady across the street until she got home. So we both waited. I called Monique and told her what was going on so she wouldn't be worried. She told me to just make sure Ezekiel was okay. I took him to get something to eat, and then we came back to the house. I told him to get his homework and I would help him. By the time it was dark, Paula arrived; higher than Mount Rushmore. Yes, I still smoked weed occasionally but nothing beyond that and cigarettes. I already knew what Paula's choice was. She tried to square up a little when she saw me. Ezekiel didn't know the difference; he had been around it so much he probably thought that was how she behaved.

It was a sad sight to see. She could barely talk, and she was grinding her teeth; it was irritating. I could only look at her. If I could have gotten away with anything else, I would have. She was Ezekiel's mother, and that made it even worse of a struggle. She said she was tired and she needed some sleep.

"Please don't leave, don't leave. I need help. You are all I got. Don't leave. I'm scared. You got some money on you?" she asked.

"Not for you and not for that," I said disturbed that she would even fix her dry mouth to ask me that.

"I need help. Please. I have been admitted to a program in Tennessee, but I don't have any way to get there. They will only hold the bed for so long," she said, still grinding her teeth.

"So how is what you're doing now supposed to help?" I asked like I already didn't know the answer.

"Okay, just don't leave. If you leave, I don't know what will happen to me." She was begging me. I stood there speechless. I didn't know why this merry-go-round with her wouldn't stop. To know Ezekiel was in the adjacent room, playing with a puppy, made my heart swell. I stepped outside to smoke a cigarette. I could have smoked one in the house, but there was enough of that going on around Ezekiel. I didn't want to do that as well. I called Monique to tell her what was going on.

"So what are *you* going to do?" she asked with an emphasis on *you*.

"I don't know. I don't want to leave Ezekiel here with this, and if I leave her, she won't ever get any help. I need his school records, and everything is closed right now." I already knew that his coming with me was going to happen. I wasn't leaving him here in this mess.

Monique was silent, and then she took a deep breath. "You do the right thing. I do understand, and I will be here when you get back," she told me with no anger, irritation, or frustration in her voice, and it was very soothing knowing that she was supporting me even in this foolishness.

"We will be there first thing in the morning after I get his records," I reassured her and said good night.

That was one of the longest nights. I sat up most of the night watching Paula wrestle with her urges. Her body wanted to get out of that house and get what it was craving. I dozed off a couple of times when I heard her snore, but as soon as I saw something move, my eyes were open. That went on all night. It was a gut-wrenching sight. Someone so intelligent, beautiful, and eloquent had been reduced to what was before me. My eyes were glad when morning came, but my body wasn't at all. I got Ezekiel up and got his clothes together. I told Paula she would have to come with us. If she was going to Tennessee and she meant what she said, I wasn't taking no for an answer. She was in no condition to argue. I would have to deal with everything when I got back to the apartment.

There was a look of disbelief on Monique's face when we showed up—me, Ezekiel, Paula, and a puppy. She could tell by the look on my face that it had been no party. We all looked tired and dirty. Not to mention we had a hyperactive puppy with us.

"We need to talk," she said, and then she mumbled something in Spanish. She had taught me a couple of words. The ones she said weren't pleasant. We went into the bedroom, and she put her hands on her hips and waved her finger at me. "You need to start talking and start talking fast. When I said to do the right thing, I meant by him, the child, not the grown mother," she hissed.

She had every right to be pissed, and I understood. But right now, at this very moment, I really didn't care. I was tired, aggravated, and overwhelmed by all these folks that kept giving me directions, and I was growing weary of the whole process.

"Look, I understand you're upset. I really do, but right now, I am tired. I am tired of this, I'm tired of her, and I am tired of having to explain myself. I told her I would help her. Doing the right thing by Ezekiel means helping her get to wherever she needs to go. I will be taking her to Tennessee as soon as I can get some rest, and you are more than welcome to come with me," I said, and I meant every word of it. I didn't care who was the oldest; it was going to be the way that I said. She looked at me and threw her hands up and mumbled again in Spanish. "That's rude, and if you are gonna cuss me out, do it in English so I will know what to say back," I said and headed for the shower.

I slept a couple of hours, and when I woke up, Monique and Paula were at the table, talking. I guessed they were cool now. We made the long trip to the VA hospital in Tennessee. We didn't take the kids. There was no need for them to go through all of that. We got there and made sure she was checked in, and then we left. The trip there was spent mostly in silence. The five-and-a-half-hour trip back was the same. That was March 2003.

By May of that same year, I was moving into my new home along with Monique and her son, Ezekiel, and Monique's dog. As usual, things went pretty smoothly, but things starting digressing rapidly. Ezekiel had gone to stay with my mother for the summer. There were arguments about this and that. She fussed because I didn't fold my boxers up in the drawer. Who folds underwear? I didn't care how I put them in the drawer. Whenever I came back, she had folded everything neatly. She fussed about this. I fussed because there was a dog in the house. Yes, it was the same dog that was in her apartment, but I didn't want the dog in the house. I didn't want her washing the dog in the same sink that the food was prepared in.

My sister and some of her coworkers came over for dinner when they were in town for training, and Monique accused me of flirting with one of my sister's friends. She started fussing at me like a child in front of them. I walk off, and she followed. When we got outside, I saw another side of her, and it didn't look too good. Then she hit me in my chest. Okay, this chick had lost her Puerto Rican mind. I stared at her and clenched my fists, only to remember she was still a female. I wasn't going to hit her, but I let it be known that if she ever put her hands on me again, I was going to forget my upbringing. Her nagging was unbearable. Her jealous tirades were increasing, and I was seeing the real Monique that had been buried for so long.

We were not in a good place after that night. Then I got sick. I went to several doctors, and they couldn't find out what was wrong. My friends that I hung out with joked me and said that Monique had roots on me. They had met her a couple of times when they came over to drink. I was referred to a gynecologist, and he examined me and had X-rays performed. I was later informed that I had severe endometriosis. I asked if the gangrene from my previous surgery may have caused it, and he said it was highly unlikely that it was caused by that. I only had a couple of options. I could have either a partial or a full hysterectomy. I told him I needed to think about it but that I would let him know. He said they would schedule the surgery as soon as I made my decision.

I listened to all that Monique had to say and looked at my life at the present moment and weighed my options. I didn't look at any of the aftereffects. I was worried about the present moment. The decision was made; it would be a full hysterectomy. The surgery was scheduled, and I was reminded of the last time I went into a hospital. One good thing was that I didn't have to worry about any of those exes showing up.

For my presurgery appointment, the doctor explained everything to expect before, during, and after the surgery. Monique went with me for the surgery; the nagging, fussing, and complaining side of her was gone. She was now concerned, motherly, and sympathetic. The doctor said it would be a simple procedure and that I'd have a short hospital stay. He was really wrong. The day after the surgery, when they removed the catheter, I developed an infection. That added five more days to my hospital stay. By the time I was released, I was miserable. I was weak and was having hot flashes repeatedly. The doctor had said I would go though menopause, but he didn't say it would be this quickly. I didn't want to be bothered most of the time. I just wanted to be by myself. When the hot flashes occurred, it was unreal. I didn't know a body could heat that quickly and then return to normal like the heat never came. They were unbearable, especially at night. I felt like I was another person and that my body was taking on a life of its own. Monique said I was becoming a monster. When I finally went back to the doctor for a follow-up and told him everything that was going on, he put me on a hormone therapy. That helped some with my moodiness but not the hot flashes. He gave me another prescription to help with those.

After about four months of that, Monique decided she'd had enough. She said my moodiness, my smoking, and all the drama were more than what she wanted to deal with. She was angry and hurt that I spent more time on the computer playing spades than talking with her. She was moving out, saying that she regretted the very day she gave me her phone number.

"You're a child that needs to grow up, and I have already raised my children. I shouldn't have to raise another one" were her final words. Her kids all came to help her pack and move all her furniture out. I wasn't going to lift a finger. It was her decision, her stuff, so her energy was going to move it.

Good riddance, and don't look back.

I should have never called her. Well, on a positive note, at least I wasn't moving this time.

The very same problems I had been having at home started surfacing at work when I returned. I was moody, temperamental, getting uncontrollable hot flashes, and crying uncontrollably at times. Then anger would take over. I remember getting so upset at a coworker that I had an anxiety attack. I was sent home. I returned to the doctor and told him something was going on, that I had no control of my emotions. They were all over the place. I would go from zero to sixty in an instant. I told him about a coworker of mine that I didn't like and that I visualized myself running him over with my vehicle every time I saw him.

"Now you don't mean that," the doctor said and looked at me to see if I was joking. He must have seen the seriousness in my face and realized I wasn't playing. "I need you to understand what you are saying, Ms. Ross."

"I meant what I said, and I said what I meant. If he called my name one more time, I was running him over," I told the doctor with emphasis.

"Ms. Ross, it is my duty as a doctor to report any incidents where someone is threatening bodily harm to someone else. I am going to have to refer you to a psychologist. You will be required to attend all sessions until you are released. If you miss your appointments or do not attend, then I will have to report this to the police," he said the last part very slowly to make sure I understood.

"I'm fine with all the above," I said, looking him squarely in the eye to make sure *he* understood.

I was sent to the mental health clinic and put on mental stress leave at work. I was listed as mentally unbalanced and a threat to others. I had to go to therapy twice a week and each time see a psychologist. I was put on more medication. One of them was oxapazem, and I hated it. I was a zombie when I took it. It was supposed to help with the anxiety attacks. Of course, it did. I was comatose half the time when I took it.

When I was not comatose, I was paranoid and hallucinating. I couldn't function. If having a hysterectomy created all this, I wondered if could the doctor put it back in. All this was not part of the plan; neither was it part of his after-surgery warnings. This teeter-totter effect went on for months. In my sober waking moments, I would play spades online.

That was where I met Camille. She could run spades like no one else. We started out as just random partners, and then we would make appointed times to play together. Before long, we were not even playing spades; we were just talking on the phone.

By the time summer came, Camille and her two teenagers were moving in. She had come for a visit once before and fell in love with the area and me. I was her first, and she said this was where she wanted to be. She was tired of the snow and the cold of the north and didn't want to stay there any longer. I believed it would help me and my emotional roller coaster as well. It had gotten better, but I wasn't the same as I was before the surgery. Maybe Monique had been putting something in my food. She did all the cooking; she insisted on it. I really couldn't afford to think about that now. If she had, the damage was already done. Camille was beautiful and funny. She made me laugh like I hadn't laughed in a long time. Ezekiel even came back for a visit during the summer, and it was wonderful.

August 9

That same summer, my phone rang, and it was my brother. I thought it was extremely odd because my brothers didn't usually call me. When I answered, I already knew something was wrong.

"Hello. What's wrong?" I asked immediately.

"You need to come home. Daddy done shot himself, and they can't get a pulse."

There was no excitement, distress, or anxiety in his voice. But that was his character—no emotions. Maybe that was why he was the one that called. I was just the opposite at that moment. I started panicking, and Camille asked me what was going on. I told her, and she said she would drive me down there. We agreed not to say anything to the kids and that they didn't need to go with us. My brother called back as we were headed down the highway to make the one-and-a-half-hour trip. He told me that they were working on Daddy and that they had a pulse. I felt like a weight was lifted from my shoulders.

When we finally arrived at the house, the yard was full of cars. This was the country. Why were all these folks in my momma's yard? I saw the sheriff's car, and I saw the "body" car. I jumped out of the car before it even stopped completely, and I ran to the porch. I was met at the door by a plainclothes officer, who told me I couldn't go into the house. Everette, my brother who called me earlier, told me I didn't want to go in there. I asked him what had happened. His voice was calm as always, but there was a look on his face that I had never seen before. The Godfather, as he was called by some, was scared and hurting.

He began to tell me that Daddy had called him and told him to come to the house so he could talk to him. He said when he got there, he was knocked at the back door and heard a gunshot. When he made it inside to the li'l den, he found him on the chair. My mother came out of the bedroom as well, and they both found him in the chair with blood pouring out of his neck. They tried to stop the bleeding, but they couldn't. I froze. I didn't know how long, and I didn't know why, but at that very moment, I felt numb. I bolted away from him and charged back toward the house, screaming, "I want to see him! I want to see him!" Why? I couldn't believe any of this was happening. This stuff happened to other folks, on TV. This time, I made it beyond the porch and into the kitchen. I was met inside by an officer in uniform this time, and she told me I couldn't go past her. I was a wreck.

"Where's my momma? Where's my momma? I want my momma!" I was thirty-six years old at the time, and I was sure my cries were that of a spoiled toddler crying for her momma.

They took me to the bedroom off to the right, where she was, but they wouldn't let me past the kitchen to go through the house to the li'l den. When I saw her sitting on the side of bed, crying, I felt a rip in my chest and knot in my stomach. She tried to assure me she was okay so I would calm down. I couldn't fall apart like this with her. My falling apart would make her fragile state even worse. I pulled myself together as best I could, for her sake. I couldn't find any words. I could only watch, and that urge to scream began to swell in me, but I suppressed it. I swallowed it back and said, *Not now.*

Something began to change in my mother's eyes, and she looked older than she had since I last saw her a few months ago. When they said they had taken the body out of the house, she began to get hysterical. Either the ambulance was already there, or it had been called, but she ended up being taken to the hospital. She stayed for observation and was released under medication and supervision. She was devastated.

After being with my mom for forty-four years, with thirty-nine of those in marriage and with nine children, this was how he left. We all were destroyed. I had to know why. I searched and looked, and when I found what I thought was the answer (because he didn't leave a note or anything; he just shot himself), I hated my daddy.

Hate is a strong word for someone who helped bring you into the world. Hate is a very strong word for someone who provided for you and eight other siblings, someone who was at all your graduations and ball games. Hate is not something you're supposed to feel for someone who taught you how to drive and bought you your first car. Hate is not supposed to go in the same sentence with the word *daddy*. All those years of me trusting him… Until that point, he was the only man I ever trusted and respected. He was the only man that had been a constant in *all* my life. After all that, he deeply traumatized the one woman I *knew* I deeply loved. Yes, the woman that had been in my life had been numerous, so many that my mom once told me that I was just as ho-ish as these boys.

Her exact words were "I don't approve of what you are doing, but if you are going to do it, do it right. Every time I see you, you got a different woman. You are just as ho-ish as these boys." She was right, and she spoke her mind at all times.

I still loved her; that had never changed. She was my heart. When he'd ripped hers, he no longer meant anything to me. Nothing.

Life after the funeral was way different for everybody. I spent my time between my momma, Camille and the kids, and work. By the spring of the following year, I was in another downward spiral. We had moved into the house that we had built on the outskirts of town. Camille had purchased the land and put it in my name, and I had the house built. It still wasn't enough. I still felt like I was just going through the motions.

They increased my meds and added a psychiatrist to my schedule at the mental health clinic. I was on another modified mental health break at work. So I had two shrinks I had to see on a regular basis. I was having trouble walking as well. When I went a specialist, my feet were the problem. My big toes were growing profusely toward my other toes, which was creating the pain from my feet up to my knees. They tried the therapeutic actions and treatment, and when that didn't work, it was surgery. This would not require a hospital stay, but it would require me to be a cast and not able to walk without crutches for six weeks.

The surgery was brief, and I was under anesthesia, so I didn't feel much. However, when the anesthesia wore off, I felt that pain. It was indescribable. I didn't understand fully what had took place until later. They had cut the bone of my big toe and reset it with some screws in order to correct the problem I had. It was then that I discovered the joy of pain pills. They were my escape from the pain, physically. The other meds were helping somewhat emotionally, but that wasn't always the case. My mom wanted to come and stay with us to make sure that I okay. I was fine with it. I felt it would be good for her to get away and to physically see I was okay. She always wanted to make sure that I was okay even after I told her that I was.

My mom came with one of my other nieces, and it was good to have them there. She was helping out, cooking and cleaning and making sure I had what I needed. Camille wasn't as happy about it as I was. My mom complained about both our cigarette smoking. I didn't pay it much mind. I ventured outside one day to find them sitting on the patio, talking, and I heard Camille telling her things about me that I would have never told my mother. Yes, my mother knew some things, but there are some things you just do not tell your mother. She told her about me smoking weed, my drinking, some of my sexual escapades, and all. I was irate.

"Why are you telling my momma all this!" I yelled.

"She's your mother, and she's needs to know what kind of daughter she has," she hissed.

"Hey, hey, hey!" my momma said, becoming the referee, "ain't no need for all that." The she began to lecture me. I tuned her out. My eyes were peered on Camille. If my mother hadn't been sitting there, I would have ripped that smug look right off her high yellow face. My feelings for her turned very quickly. I no longer saw her beauty, but I saw how ugly she had become. She wasn't happy, and she would rather see me miserable and hurt my mother in the process. I got up from the table and hobbled back into the house on my crutches. She had crossed the line, and there was no coming back. After my mom finally left, she felt my wrath. The arguments increased, and so did my anger. I began smoking more, and I knew it was a deadly combination on the meds.

I then started hearing voices at times when no one was around. Sometimes they were whispers, like multitudes of folks, and sometimes they were very loud. Camille and I had our moments, but the bad ones were really bad. I had to have the surgery on my other foot by the time the cast came off the other foot, and I was allowed to walk on it. All together it was over four months that I was in that house with her day in, day out, and it was a nightmare.

I saw this movie once called *Beloved* a while back. It was about a woman and her family who were haunted by the ghost of a baby she had killed to keep her from being a slave. Camille reminded me of that ghost at times. She actually looked like the woman in the movie, and at times, when she was angry, her voice sounded ghostly and demonic. I was worn out. I wanted out so bad, but I refused to go out like my daddy did. I thought about it at times, but I could never make myself swallow enough of the pills.

I remember walking around in the backyard, and there was a church across the road with only one car there. I walked across to see if anyone was there, and the pastor and his wife were there. I remembered her from when I worked at DFCS. She was glad to see me, and from nowhere, everything I had gone though just started bubbling out. The pastor told me they would pray with me and that everything would be okay. I left afterward, but I didn't feel any better. I remembered as I was walking back home that the electrician who had wired the house was a preacher and that I had gone to a church in town to hear him speak as a guest.

That next Sunday, I went to the church in town. It was called Walls of Grace, and I enjoyed the service so much that I wanted to join. I spoke to the pastor and his wife and told them my story. I told them that I was tired of what I was doing and needed help. They offered their support in whatever I needed. In my mind, this was the right thing to do. I went home and told Camille about everything. She said she wanted the same thing and that she would go with me the next time, she and the kids. The next Sunday, we all went, but when it was time for altar call, she didn't move. She sat back down and just stared.

When we got back home, she said I was crazy and blind. "You can't see what they are doing? They are brainwashing you, and you are too stupid or high to see it." Her eyes were piercing when she said it, and drops of spittle formed on the corners of her mouth.

Yeah, you are crazy, I thought. *I am in the house with someone who is haunting me in my thoughts and in my face.*

When she saw I wasn't responding or talking, she threw her hands up in the air and walked out. I had to leave—no ruminating with this one. I wished I had never given up my first house. This time, it was going to be costly. Everything was in my name—house, new vehicle, utilities. *Everything*. At that moment, I didn't care. I just wanted out. I went back to church a couple of times, but I gave up on that within a couple of months. Nothing in the house was really changing. There would be good moments, and then there would be horrible moments.

Money was getting tighter and tighter. While I was out for the surgeries, my pay got screwed up, and everything fell behind. Camille wasn't working. As a matter of fact, she hadn't worked since I met her. Her only income was child support and the residuals from her mom's insurance policy after she died. She got a job, but it didn't last long. By April of 2006, I had to file for bankruptcy. I could keep the house we were living in but lost everything else.

I felt myself on that merry-go-round again, the one that never stopped to let me off no matter how hard I screamed to get off. It wouldn't ever stop. Crying was not an option. I didn't even cry at funerals. I just had this voice in my head that always wanted to scream all the time. My smoking increased. The mental health visits were really not helping, but I hadn't been released. Camille even went with me to a couple of them. She must have thought I was lying

166

when I kept leaving the house. I wasn't happy, and neither was she. She let it be known, and so did I.

I moved out of that haunted house and in with a close friend and a coworker of mine. He said he understood what I was going through emotionally and financially, and until I got myself straight, I could stay there as long as I needed. There was only one rule. What goes on in his house stays in his house. I had no problem with that. I understood he was single, so I let his business be his. I was just glad to be out of that house with "beloved." Unfortunately, since the house was still in my name, I was obligated to pay the house note. That was where it started getting tricky. I could never get my own place as long as I had a $800 house note. I told Camille we needed to sell it or I would just take the hit and let it foreclose. She turned three colors through the phone. I didn't care. I wasn't in it. It could catch a fire for all I cared.

Initially, I had moments of regret, but that all changed when it was time for the house to be sold. She had gotten a lawyer, and I would not be allowed to get the proceeds from the sale since I "abandoned" the house. The sale of the house would be around $225,000. The bank would get $144,000 for the loan, I would get only $5,000, the rest would be hers. I understood now that this was her plan all the long. I had a choice—to take the $5,000 or be connected to her even longer. I was done, and I had been outdone. I didn't want to repeat the cycle, so I decided to do something different.

That Sunday, I went back to the church that I had last visited. I hadn't been there in six months, and I was embarrassed to even go back. I went in and sat down in the back. I hardly recognized anyone that was there. When the preacher got up to preach, I recognized him from work.

He must be the guest speaker, I thought to myself.

Service was wonderful. I greeted the preacher, and he said he was glad to see me. I asked him if he would be back, and he said yes, that it was his church.

"You didn't see the sign outside?" he asked.

I shook my head no and wondered what was he talking about. When I finally went outside, I saw that this was the same building that I had went to earlier in the year, but it was a different church membership. I laughed at myself. I was that distraught and that far gone that I didn't even realize I was in the wrong church. I kept coming back. I even joined the praise team. Things were getting better. I just still needed to get rid of my smoking habit. It had decreased a lot, but it wasn't gone. This was what I needed.

I started going to church regularly and met some wonderful folks but no real friends to socialize with. After church, everyone went their separate ways. Here and there, Camille would send me a harassing email, but I was done with her. My housemate had his own life, and he wasn't gonna babysit me. I was getting bored, and so I decided to change my hair. It was growing out from the faded cut I always wore, and it was at an ugly stage where I couldn't do anything with it. I never was a hair person. I didn't know how to do anything other than put it in a ponytail. Right now, that wasn't an option. It wasn't even long enough to pull together. I had a mini Afro. One day at work, I saw one of the housekeeping staff with a lovely hairstyle with micro braids in the front and long curly hair in the back. I stopped her and asked her who her hairstylist was, and she told me it was her niece. She gave me her number and said to call her and that she would do mine as well.

I called the number as soon as I returned to my office. I told her who I was and how I came across her number. I expressed my interest in getting my hair done, but I didn't know if I had enough hair on my head to get what I wanted. She told me I could stop by and she would take a look at it and see what she could do with it. I went by her apartment after work, and she said it wouldn't be a problem catching my short hair. She told me where to go get the hair and made my appointment.

X9

<hr /> ++++++ <hr />

May 2007

Vanessa had been doing my hair for over six months now, and we had become good friends. She said I was like the mother she never had. She was about twelve years younger than I was, and she said I brought a little light into the house. She liked hearing me talk about the church and all the things at work. I would hang out sometimes with her and her four kids. She had girls. Her boyfriend would always ask me about selling my truck. He didn't talk that much, but every once in a while, he would say a few words to me. I was becoming part of their family. Sometimes I would go and just sit and talk and watch her do her hair just to have something to do, and I started going more and more. I began to hang out with her and her sisters, and I never saw what was coming, but I felt it. I was becoming more and more attracted to her. I was still going to church, singing on the praise team and all these things that I was supposed to be doing, but the feelings started creeping back.

I didn't understand any of it. I had changed my hair, my clothes. I was getting my nails done, and still nothing had really changed. The craziest part about it was that it wasn't just me. I saw the look she would get in her eyes when it was time for me to leave. There was a sadness that came across them. I saw the smile that she gave me when I walked in the door. I felt like this was where I was supposed to be. I was going to church, and I met someone who was innocent, not playing games, not scheming or plotting, and she was interested in me even without me looking the way I had been all these years. I took that as a sign that I was sent there for a reason, but I was getting the signals mixed up. As hard as I tried to pull on the brakes, I couldn't. I had fallen for her, and it wasn't just her. I felt like I had been blessed with a family I would never have on my own.

By July of that year, we had crossed the line. We were no longer just friends. I was no longer viewed as a mother figure. The breakup with her boyfriend was horrible and less than drama free, but that was her decision. She wanted to be with me, and I didn't want any third parties. I was called a home wrecker. My attendance at church had become nonexistent. I was back to what I knew as familiar, and this time, I wasn't leaving. I had a family, and I felt needed and wanted.

The first five or six months weren't baby daddy drama free. Vanessa dealt with it pretty good. I got the mean looks whenever he came around and saw me. It didn't bother me one bit. It was funny how folks wouldn't do what they were supposed to do when they were in the house but as soon as someone else was there, they wanted to be picture-perfect. I didn't move in the apartment with her and the kids immediately. That was both our decision; it was because of the kids. I was the first woman she had been with, and all the girls had ever known was their daddy. I respected that, but I didn't care at all for baby daddy or anything with the name of daddy. The pain from the man that had been married to my mother for all those years still cut deep. Every time I saw a picture of him, I frowned. Ugh. But that would not spoil this relationship.

We began to travel to different places together. I would rent a vehicle that would hold all of us, and we would go. My "flaming" truck wasn't a family-oriented vehicle. Eventually, the flaming truck had to go, and I upsized to a family vehicle. I didn't officially move into the apartment, but I was living there enough. It was a whirlwind of good times.

By November of 2008, we have moved into a house. We actually thought about buying, but due to my recent bankruptcy, that was not an option. She found a house for rent, and it was perfect. It had a large backyard that was fenced in, and best of all, it would be ours. We were happy, still not baby daddy drama free, but I was used to it by now. Pretty soon, everyone got used to seeing us as a family—my family, her family. We all were one big unit.

I was no longer having to go the mental clinic, and I was glad. The only med I had to take was the hormone pills. I couldn't function without those. I made the mistake of allowing my prescription to lapse, and by day three, I couldn't even think. I was severely depressed and was moving in slow motion. I could barely get out of bed. I knew not to make that mistake again. I sometimes wondered why it took me so long to get to this place and why none of the other relationships were this simple. Even with four kids, it wasn't as complicated as all my exes. We talked of growing old together. I tried as best as I could to make her life simple. I was saddened when she talked about her upbringing and all the things she had gone through. I wanted to be her angel. I realized that all this time we had been together, we had never had an argument. We didn't yell or fuss at each other. Yeah, okay, she would get mad sometimes and say what she had to say and be done, but she didn't nag or whine.

After many birthdays, field day events, hairdos for the girls, family trips, backyard BBQs, and questions, the girls grew before my eyes, and I was a part of it. They were old enough to actually understand the relationship I had with their mother, and they were unbothered. There were all those typical growing pain moments. I couldn't say we were perfect, but they didn't last long or create a bridge between any of us. Before I knew it, four years had passed by in that house, and it all seemed like it had only been a couple of months. We had gotten into a groove, a good one. Paula had even tried to pop up and create the usual ruckus, but that was diffused really quickly. Vanessa wasn't about the foolishness, and I didn't blame her.

Sunday, January 1, 2012

It was the beginning of a new year, and I was looking forward to many more New Years with Vanessa and the girls. By that Monday, I was not too sure. I got a call from Macy's girlfriend that Macy had died. I hadn't had a blow to my heart like that since I got that phone call from my brother eight years ago.

"What! Noooooooooooo! Please don't tell me that!" I was hurt. I was confused. I was in shock.

"Yeah, she died last night from complications from pneumonia," she said. "I can't really talk about it right now, but I will get back to you with the details," she said and then hung up the phone before I could say anything else.

My road dog was dead. She had sent me a text around the first part of December, telling me that she was in the hospital, but she never said why. I told her that I would come to visit, but I never made it up there. When I never heard back from her, I figured she was out and back to her usual. We both had our own families, so it wasn't like we talked every day. Vanessa and I had gone over to their house for a party a few months before that to hang out and play spades, and she looked fine.

I was scratching my head and looking for answers in my dreadlocks, but nothing came. I walked back into the house, and Vanessa looked at me and asked what was wrong.

"Macy died last night."

Her gasp was all I needed to hear. I walked into the bedroom and closed the door. For the first time in so long, I cried. We had been through a lot together. It didn't matter when I called or what I asked her to do; she was down for it. This couldn't be happening. The week found me staring into space a lot. I was quiet more than usual and slightly withdrawn. Vanessa said she understood what I was going though and wished that she could help. The only thing that could help me with this was for it to be not true. I had lost plenty of relatives, coworkers, other friends, and classmates. But this one right here took the cake. I had known her for almost fifteen years, and she was always the same Macy. Me? I was moody at times. But she was always good for laughs. She was the life of every party, and boy, did we party. That life had been removed.

Vanessa went with me to the funeral. She said she was worried about me and that she could see how this was tearing me apart. I sat there at the funeral and saw all these people that we used to hang out with, and it was really sad. Then the craziest thought popped into my mind while I was sitting there. I wondered if my mother would put me in a dress when I died. I had been wearing men's clothing for years. Would my mother put me in a dress and have them put makeup on me? Then the truth really struck home. That meant I would have to be dead.

Oh my, I don't want to die like this.

The next few weeks were about the same. I did start seeing some improvement, but death, the thoughts surrounding my death, and everything I was hearing in my mind started bothering me. I dismissed it all and dug in a little deeper into everything. I stayed busy around the house and worked. By June, I was good and ready to move on. My niece was getting married, and we were going to the wedding. Plans changed slightly when Cody showed up. Cody was the six-month-old cousin who came over for a visit and never left. We all loved him. He was the first boy that was in the house. The kids and I went to the wedding, and Vanessa stayed at home with Cody.

The wedding was beautiful. My niece was gorgeous, and her husband smiled the biggest smile when she walked down the aisle. I saw how he looked in her eyes and she looked into his, and I felt a small tinge of jealousy. I wanted that. I must have been really drunk or my meds were not functioning properly. I wanted a wedding. I dismissed that thought as quick as I could. There were four young ladies sitting beside me and one grown one at the house that ruled all that out. Next!

The fall and winter was our favorite time of the year. Vanessa and I would sit out in the yard and burn a fire in the barrel and just chill. I was feeling a little better from the earlier part of the year, but I still felt slightly disconnected. Vanessa said that she noticed I was changing, but I didn't see it. I didn't want to be touched, and our sex life had become almost nonexistent. I couldn't explain it, and I didn't try. We still talked and went about our usual activities, and I tried to ignore it. I told her I was going to give up smoking. I had said that sooooooo many times, but this time, I meant it. She looked me like "Yeah, okay." I had already stopped drinking a long time ago. The alcohol and the hormone pill for some reason didn't mix, and eventually, I lost the taste for it.

One September evening, I was standing out at the burn barrel, smoking, and I heard a very distinctive and clear voice say, "It's time." I looked around; there was no one there but me. My heart began to feel really heavy, and I felt a pull. I knew what that meant. A part of me wanted to shake my head and make the voice and what was said go away, but I couldn't.

I never said anything to Vanessa about it, but by the end of the week, I told her I was going to church Sunday.

"Okay, we can all go as a family," she said.

"Not this time. Maybe next week. I need to go by myself," I told her. I didn't know what to expect, and I knew I hadn't been to that church since I left over five years ago. I hadn't been there for so long that I didn't know what time service started. I texted the pastor's phone number that I had and checked to see what time service started, and he told me it started at ten.

When Sunday came, I put on my blue linen suit and went to church. When I walked in the door of the church, I felt lighter. As I stepped in the door of the sanctuary, a feeling of guilt rushed all over me. I slowly made my way to the last row and sat down. Service had already started, and so had my tears. I cried and cried the entire time while the praise team was singing. When it was time for prayer, all I could do was fall on my knees at my chair and say over and over "Forgive me, forgive me." My heart and head were heavy, and the more I cried and cried for forgiveness, the better I felt. By the time the pastor stepped on stage to deliver the Word, I knew there was no going back this time.

Every word he spoke that day I felt was directed at me. This wasn't the pastor that was here before. This was a guest pastor, so I knew I didn't know him and he didn't know me, but his words went through to me.

When he was through preaching, he asked if anyone wanted to come to the altar for salvation, prayer, or any need. I walked forward slowly. My feet seemed to get heavier as I made my way to the altar. I saw some familiar faces, and they were all smiling. As I stood at the altar, the pastor who had preached came closer to me.

"My child, what is your sin?" he whispered.

I was silent. My mind told me to tell him "Can't you look at me and tell?" But I didn't say it. I knew what my sin was; I had known all these years. I was attracted to women. Some I loved. Some I didn't. I knew it, God knew it, and everybody in this church knew it. Half the city of Albany knew it. Everybody on my job knew it. My family knew it. What they didn't know was that I was sick of it. I wanted off this merry-go-round. It always ended up in the same place. The difference this time was that no one was pushing me off. *I wanted off!* I didn't want to die like this.

"It's already done," he whispered in my ear without me ever saying a word. My tears were enough. He looked me in the eyes and said it again and again, "It's already done."

One of the other ministers that I could remember from before came and hugged me and said, "Welcome back."

As I returned to my seat, I didn't feel heavy. My head felt clearer, and my body felt lighter. After service, I made my exit. I had to deal with what was waiting for me when I returned home. Vanessa had to go to work, so I told her that we needed to talk when she got home.

That night, I was worried but not afraid. I knew that this was something I could not run away from again or change my mind about. My heart was being drawn somewhere else, and it wasn't toward another woman. When she got home that night and the kids had gone to bed, I started telling her about that day at church.

"I need you to know that I do love you and the kids very much, but there's something else I have to do. I can't do this anymore. When I met you, I was in the church, and I messed up what I was supposed to be doing. We crossed the line. But I take full responsibility for it because I knew better. I know it hurts, and it hurts me as well. But I can't, and we can't go on together." I tried to explain, but every word I said dug deeper and deeper. I saw that hurt in her eyes that I used to see when I would leave her apartment. It stung.

She tried to hold back the tears, but they started. She jumped off the bed and headed out the bedroom. "I'm gonna sleep on the sofa" was all I heard before the door closed.

Okay, now what? I asked myself.

I wasn't going in there. She needed her time to process everything. I needed time to process everything. We spent a lot of time over the next few weeks talking and crying. There were moments of silence as well, but I believed we both knew what was happening was not going to be undone. I told her that I wouldn't just walk out. I wanted to her to understand that I took into consideration that there were five kids to consider, but I would look for another place. She understood and said that there was no rush, I could do whatever I needed to do. I reassured her that I would give her enough advance notice before I left so she could be prepared to take over the bills.

PATRICIA ANDERSON

I went to church every Sunday. I even started going to Bible study. I was back on the praise team and was moving in the right direction. I started buying some ladies' clothing from Goodwill to wear to church so I wouldn't be going in men's clothing. My search for somewhere to stay was not going very well. By the end of November, two months later, I found a house and put in an application to buy it. I didn't talk to Vanessa about it. I was waiting for the approval from the loan company first. We were not in a bad place with each other, and things were good. I was approved for a loan, and I put an offer on the house.

Saturday December 8, 2012

The praise team had another singing event to participate in at a church outside of Americus. I drove and met the others there. The small church was packed, and we were the last ones to go up and sing. We sang our songs, and when we finished the last song, we returned to our seats. Then our praise team leader turned back around and picked up the microphone and started singing again. We all joined in singing from our seats, and he would not stop. I sat there looking, and the room began to become hazy. I looked into his eyes as he was singing, and there was a fire in his eyes. The first lady started running up and down the aisle, shouting, and there were other people shouting. The whole room appeared to be happy, and I was amazed.

When he finally finished, one of the ministers began to speak, and she made a call to come to the altar. A few others and myself walked to the front. As I was standing there, the minister began to pray. I stood there for quite a while, and I thought this was an unusually long prayer. I was always taught to bow my head and close my eyes, so I did, and I kept them closed as long as I could.

And then I heard a low whisper: "Watch the demons move." I peeked out the corner of my right eye, and I saw some people backing away from the altar. That same voice whispered again, "Don't move."

I didn't move from that spot, but I slowly lifted my head and saw that a woman wasn't praying but was talking to people individually. More and more people were backing away, and I stood there as the voice had whispered for me not to move. The minister was to my right, talking to someone. She passed right by me and went to the person on my left. When she finished, that person went to the next person on their left. She started back in my direction, and then she walked past me. She then made a sudden stop and came back to me and looked me straight in my eyes.

She said, "You already know. You already know. You've been running and fighting, but you already know. You have work to do. God has something for you to do, and if anybody tries to stand in your way, you let Him deal with them. You don't have to explain to anyone what He has told you to do."

I fell to my knees. I had never seen this woman before in my life, but she knew! No, she didn't know, but God did. She was still talking to me, but I couldn't and didn't hear anything else. I was on my knees, crying again. After a while, she told me to stand up, and she asked me my name. She told me to turn around and face the congregation.

As soon as I turned around, she said, "Brothers and sisters, I introduce to some and present to others the new Elaine Ross."

I was moved and, at the same time, questioning, *What did I already know?*

After service, I left without talking to anyone. I needed to think. As I was driving back to the house, my mind was replaying all the events and trying to figure out what I already knew.

Ding! I had on men's underwear!

I was wearing ladies clothing, but I still had on boxer briefs. I didn't own any ladies' underwear. I needed new underwear. That was it! When I got to Albany, I went straight to Wal-Mart. I went to the ladies' department and looked for some underwear. As I stood there looking, I felt embarrassed. I hadn't worn panties in so long that I didn't even know what size to wear or what kind to buy. I did the math according to the size boxer briefs I had been buying and used the waist measurement to narrow it down. Well, now what kind? There were so many. I just picked five different styles and went to the cash register. I made it back to the house, and Vanessa was still at work. I went into the room and closed the door. I pulled off my clothes, pulled off the briefs, and put on a pair of the panties.

When I pulled them up around my hips, my body said, *Whew!* It was if this was what my butt had been missing.

I put on my pajamas and sat down, and that same voice whispered, "That's not it."

I asked, "What else?"

Then the answer came: "You already know."

I walked over to the dresser and started pulling out all the clothes and piling them on the floor. By the time I was finished, the only things left in the dresser were my sports bras, socks, and panties. I looked at the pile. "That's not it. You already know." I went to the closet and started pulling out clothes and piling them on the floor as well. Everything had to go.

I spoke out loud, "I need something to wear to work."

The voice replied, "T-shirts, jeans, and a few tennis shoes."

While I was going through the closet, Vanessa came in and looked.

"What are you doing with those?" she asked.

"Throwing them out—unless you know someone who can wear them," I said with no explanation.

"Put them in a bag, and I will give them to somebody," she said, and she walked back out of the room.

I looked at the closet. It was practically empty. I only had enough clothes left for one work week. Before I went to bed that night, I began to pray. I still felt like there was something else that I was missing. When I prayed, I asked for whatever it was that I already knew, that I hadn't done to be made known. I went to bed. I slept that well that night, better than I had slept in a while. I remember dreaming and seeing myself asleep in a huge cloud that was the shape of an arm. It was so white and comfortable, and I felt love! And truly loved.

Sunday December 9, 2012

My eyes flew open, and I sat up straight in the bed. *I gotta get out of this house!* Panic then set in. That was what I already knew!

Yes, the clothes and all that were a part of it, but the biggest thing was that I needed to get out of the house! It was still very early in the morning, and I had nowhere to go. The offer hadn't been accepted on the house, and I hadn't looked anywhere else. I called my mother. I explained to her everything that had happened last night. I didn't tell her much of anything else other than that because she had been down this road with me before, and I didn't want to hear that speech. She told me I could come stay with her and we would figure it out.

"Momma, that's an hour and a half of one-way commute to work. That's too far for me to drive and to go to church. I will think about it. Let me call Minister Sims and let her know what's going on. I may not make it this morning." I hung up the phone and called Minister Sims.

Minister Sims was over at the music ministry, and we were told to call her if we weren't going to be at rehearsal or church. She and I had talked quite a few times church, and she was an extremely nice lady. I called her and tried to explain everything that had happened since yesterday. She had not attended the service in Americus and did not know what had happened. I told her that I had to move from where I staying and why. She already knew about my living arrangement. She knew I was waiting to hear about the house. She told me to go ahead and get dressed and come to church. She said she would talk to her husband and see what they could come up with.

"You just come to church" were her last words.

I did as I was told. I sat in Sunday school, almost in tears. I made it through service, but still there was no word from Minister Sims.

When service was over, she came up to me and said, "He said okay. You can come stay with us." She smiled. "Go and get your stuff, and come over after you're done. I will text you the address." She hugged me and told me not to worry, that it was going to be okay.

X10

When I first stepped into the Sims' house, I felt like I was in heaven. The air was clean, and I could smell a sweet aroma all over. It was extremely bright even with the lights off. Mr. Sims helped me get my belongings off the truck. When he brought my clothes into the house to put them in the closet, I could smell my clothes. They were clean. Well, they had been washed, but they smelled like wet cigarettes and mildew. I never knew clean clothes could smell so bad. He must have noticed as well, but he told me not to worry, that we would get them cleaned up. I was embarrassed. As soon as he walked out the room, I sniffed the blouse I had on, and sure enough, all my clothes smelled like that.

Now I knew of them, but I didn't really know them. Minister Sims and his wife were both ministers at the church. I saw them, and I had talked with her a couple of times, but beyond that, I had no clue who they were. I was not going to complain. They were giving me shelter until I closed on the house. It was weird being in the house with strangers, and I was sure they felt the same about me. I was one yes away from being homeless. Actually, I was homeless.

Whatever had to be done, I knew I couldn't stay in that house another night with Vanessa and the kids. They hadn't done anything wrong, and we all were hurting. But the voice had spoken. I was no longer following my own mind. After all my stuff had been unloaded, we sat in the living room to eat and talk. They did most of the talking. I explained to them that I was waiting to hear from the inspector regarding the house. I was expecting to close within a month. Everything I owned I already had it with me except two other vehicles. I was leaving one with Vanessa. All the furniture, TVs, and anything else was hers as well. I had the few items of clothes, shoes, and some laundry detergent. I was starting from scratch. I knew eventually the clothes I had brought with me would even have to go. They reassured me that it was no rush and that I was more than welcome to stay and feel free to ask any questions that I had. I didn't have any. I was tired. But there was another service that we had to go to at church, so there would be no rest yet.

Monday December 10, 2012

After work, I found out that there was an issue with the house. Apparently, the seal underneath was rotten, and there were electrical issues. The repairs would totaling to about $13,000. I told Mrs. Sims about it, and she asked me where the hoses was located.

I described the location, and she quickly asked, "Next door to that palm reader?" Her face was serious.

"Yes, ma'am," I answered curiously.

"Oh no, ma'am. You don't need that anyways. That is not somewhere you need to live. I will check tomorrow when I go to work. I believe I know someone who has a house for sale, and I will check to see if it's still available. No, it's a good thing that it needs work. You won't be moving there," she said and shook her head.

I didn't understand why it put her on guard like it did. I just accepted what she said even though I was disappointed. Mr. Sims came home and called me into his office. He gave me some scriptures to read, and I told him about the house as well. He agreed with his wife and said that I had time; there was no rush. That night, before I went to bed, I read the scriptures he gave me.

I started hearing the voice again: *Pray and obey.* I listened until I fell asleep.

Tuesday December 12, 2012

I went to work slightly tired. I wasn't getting much sleep. I would wake up at all times in the middle of the night and read the Bible. I placed it on the bed beside me so it would be right there when I did have to wake up. When I got to the Sims' after work, Mrs. Sims was in the kitchen, cooking, and we talked for a while. We were all trying to learn from one another. After we had eaten, I took a shower and said I was going to lie down. I fell asleep and then woke up, looking around to see where I was. I heard that voice: *Read.* I didn't know what to read, but I had a very weird feeling, like the beginning of an anxiety attack. I was looking for a particular scripture about testing the spirits and couldn't find it. I ended up at Philippians 4. While I was a reading, Mrs. Sims knocked and opened the door and asked if I was okay. I waved to her and showed her that I was reading. She backed out of the room quietly. I got to verse 10, and the subtitle said, "Thanks for Their Gifts."

"I rejoiced greatly in the Lord that at last you renewed your concern for me. Indeed, you were concerned, but you had no opportunity to show it. I am not saying this because I am in need, for I have learned to be content whatever the circumstances. I know what it is to be in need, and I know what it is to have plenty. I have learned the secret of being content in any and every situation, whether well fed or hungry, whether living in plenty or in want. I can do all this through him who gives me strength. Yet it was good of you to share in my troubles. Moreover, as you Philippians know, in the early days of your acquaintance with the gospel, when I set out from Macedonia, not one church shared with me in the matter of giving and receiving, except you only; for even when I was in Thessalonica, you sent me aid more than once when I was in need. Not that I desire your gifts; what I desire is that more be credited to your account" (Philippians 4:10–17).

I wanted to shout when I read the scripture, but it was late, and I didn't want to scare Mr. and Mrs. Sims. I kept saying over and over to myself, "I'm in the right place. I'm in the right place."

I said another prayer and went back to sleep. I didn't how long I was asleep, but I felt someone in the room with me. I tried to scream, but I couldn't open my mouth. I felt something holding my mouth closed. When I looked toward the door, I saw two evil-looking creatures coming toward me, and they both had long knives in their hands. Both of their eyes were on fire, and I screamed.

When I sat up in the bed, I was sweating. I jumped out of bed and started crying and talking to myself. "I got it wrong. I got it wrong! I gotta get out of this house!" I was frightened. I ran out of the room and knocked on the Sims' bedroom door. Mrs. Sims finally came to the door half asleep, asking me what was the matter.

"There's something in my room!" I said, shaking as I said it.

In a very calm and slow voice, she said as she looked at me with her eyes half open, "All that is, is the enemy trying to attack you and get you to go back to where you once were. It is nothing to be afraid of." Her tone didn't change.

I stood there looking and tapping back and forth, thinking to myself, *Lady, you don't know what I just saw in that room!* I was shaking my head back and forth, and I felt the tears forming. I guessed she saw I was serious and wasn't moving.

"Hold on. Let me get my husband." She closed the door.

I didn't care what she said. I was not going back into that room. Those things were real!

Mr. Sims came to the door and I told him the same thing. He led me back into the room and started saying something and reading some scripture, but he didn't understand the image that would not leave my head. I started rocking from side to side, feeling the anxiety swelling on the inside. I didn't know what he said or read, but after he finished, he asked me a question.

"Do you want to be made whole?" He stood there looking at me, and I didn't really understand what he meant, but if being made whole would make those things I saw go away, then I was all for it.

"Yes! Yes!" I couldn't say it fast enough.

He asked me to raise both my hands, and he started saying something I didn't understand and tapping both my hands as they were raised. Mrs. Sims came into the room, speaking a language I didn't understand and slinging oil all around the room. When they both were finished, he began to explain to me some things that I might experience or feel in the upcoming days. I didn't understanding anything. I just wanted those images to not return. When they finally left the room, I turned the TV and watched the Christian Broadcast Channel. From that night on, I went to bed with the TV on all night—something I never could do before. I needed to see anything that walked around in that room.

That Wednesday, Thursday, and Friday day and night were all the same. I went to work, went to the Sims' house, talked, ate, read the Bible, and then no sleep for me. I would spend most of the night reading or watching the Christian Broadcast Channel. If I did fall asleep, I would be awakened with the overwhelming urge to read the Bible, pray, or watch whatever was broadcasting on that channel. Sometimes I would feel little things jumping up and down on the bed, or I would see something walking around the room. I couldn't sleep, and I never turned the TV from that channel. It was as if I had no control over my body. I could feel my head being turned toward the television or my eyes being pulled open to read. I didn't fight it.

Saturday, December 15, 2012

I went to visit my mom. I had tried to convince over the phone that I was okay and I had somewhere to stay. She wasn't hearing it. She wanted to lay her eyes on me. When she did, she was overjoyed. We talked almost all day, and then I had to leave. I couldn't stay the night. I had to get to church in the morning. I went back to the Sims', and we talked some more. I was exhausted. I took a shower and went into the room. I was watching a movie about a girl who had lost her dad and how he came back as an angel and she forgave him. It reminded me of the conversation my mother and I had regarding my dad. For some reason, she had brought him up in our conversation, saying how she had to forgive him for what he did and that she had realized that it was the only way she could move on. The movie that I was watching was talking about the same thing.

When the movie ended, it was late, but I couldn't fall asleep. I got up out of bed and began to pray. I began to feel weird, and I starting talking to my dad. I told him that I forgave him and that I could no longer hate him for what he had done to momma or the rest of us. I might never know the reason why he did, and I no longer wanted to know the reason, but he was forgiven. As I was praying, like I always did, with my eyes closed, I saw a light flickering behind my closed eyes. I refused to open my eyes, but the light kept flickering, like a fluorescent bulb going bad. I tightened my eyes and saw these two huge blue hands coming from above and reaching down as if they were trying to pull me up. They looked like thousands of blue stars gathered together to form hands. I started lifting up my hands toward those hands, but before I could reach them, they disappeared. I ended my prayer and got into bed to read. I was shaken by what I had just seen but not terrified.

Before I started reading, I began to feel weird. It felt like the beginning of a panic attack. My mother always told me that whenever I felt scared or needed help, I should just say Psalm 23. I opened my mouth to say it loud, but I couldn't remember it. Now I knew for a fact that it was the only scripture I ever memorized in my life. I gave up on the recitation from memory and turned to the scripture in the Bible. That weird feeling was intensifying. When I found the scripture, I tried to read it out loud but couldn't utter a sound. My breathing was becoming labored. I took a deep breath and pointed my finger to each and every word and forced my mouth to pronounce them. When I finally got to the end of the entire scripture, I started back over again. I kept repeating it over and over, and then it became a rhythm. Before I knew it, I heard hundreds of voices saying it aloud with me over and over. I started to doze off, but my head shot up. *Not yet.* I went back through it repeatedly. I began to doze off, but my eyes flew open. *Not yet.* Over and over and over, I repeated the scripture: "The Lord is my shepherd. I shall not want..."

I felt my entire body being lifted like a rag doll. Something was pulling my body up toward the ceiling. Then all of a sudden, I was being thrown all around the room. My body was spinning around and around like something in a horror movie. I started screaming!

"Jesus! Jesus! Jesus! Jeeesuuussssss!"

It threw me repeatedly from wall to wall and sent me in circles me, and I screamed even louder.

"Jesusssssss! Jesus! Jesus! Jesus."

Then *it* threw me against the wall face first and pinned me to the wall. The wall then became a mirror, and I saw myself in the mirror. But it wasn't all of my face as I knew it. It was my body figure, my features, my hair, but the eyes were demonic. There were empty black pits with a red beam in the middle of each one.

When I saw that face, I screamed, "Jesus! Oh, Jesus! Jesus! Jesus, Jesus!" And then I looked in the mirror again and saw a small blue light in the far distance in the rear of my head, and I yelled, "Jesussssssssssssssss!" I kept screaming Jesus's name, and the more I screamed, the closer that blue light came until it reached the front of my face. When it came to inches to my face, the thing that was holding me immediately released me. *It* tried to pick me back up again, but it couldn't. It dropped me again, and my eyes flew open.

I was still in the bed. I could only move my eyes for a moment. My entire body was paralyzed. I looked down, and my hand still on the scripture "Yea though I walk through the valley of the shadow of death, I will fear no evil; for thou art with me; thy rod and thy staff they comfort me. Surely goodness and mercy shall follow me all the days of my life: and I will dwell in the house of the LORD for ever." I knew beyond the shadow of a doubt that I had been delivered from the hands of the enemy.

*****

I have been free goin' on eight years, and it is *amazing* when I look at where I once was and where I am now. For twenty-five years, I was on a path of destruction, and I didn't even realize it. I was looking for true love and for someone to truly love me. But how could they love me when I didn't even love myself? I didn't know my identity, and I was always trying to be what the other person's image was of me. I was a chameleon, hiding in my own skin and at times not even liking who I had become. I allowed bitterness, hurt, and anger to lead me in my decisions. Yes, there were some that I loved and some that I didn't. There were some that had faces and no names. I was hurting deep, and in return, I hurt *a lot* of people. I justified hurting them by whatever actions they did to uphold me in my errors. The one that I chose to be completely honest in, God, pulled me out of that.

Completely honest? That's an oxymoron. I still wasn't honest with myself—maybe to them, but not myself. I had chosen something that I did not understand fully, but I knew in my deepest place that it was wrong. I struggled for so long, trying to do it on my own, and I would always end up back on that "merry-go-round" again. Each time, it was worse than before and harder to get away from. As long as I was deciding, I was stuck in my own dark place, and as result, I introduced this darkness to many people.

I was spreading it around like cancer, consuming and destroying whatever I touched. I felt obligated when I had done so and never realized that even after the introduction, they had a choice just like I did. For whatever the reason may have been—molestation, anger, bitterness, betrayal, perversion, being needy, being loveless, or being in search of something—at the end of the day, it was still a *choice*.

I chose the women, the drugs, the alcohol. It wasn't until my heart started changing and I was truly being honest with myself that my mind changed as well and allowed a genuine change to take place. God, in all his graciousness, rescued me, and my commitment to him is to do the same. Just like I was spreading that darkness, I am committed to spreading His light all the more—times ten.

I pray that someone will read this and know that they, too, have a choice and they, too, can be delivered.

It doesn't matter how long you have been out there or what you have done. There is a always a chance as long as you believe.

2014

2016

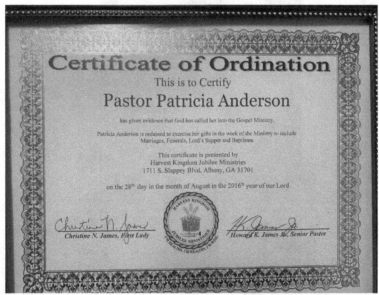

2018

PATRICIA ANDERSON

2019

2019

2020

About the Author

———— ⋆ ✦ ✦ ◆ ✦ ✦ ⋆ ————

Patricia Anderson is the founding pastor of Emmanuel—New Beginnings Ministries in Dixie, Georgia. She currently resides in Albany, Georgia, with her loving husband, who supports her in the ministry of teaching, preaching, and dance.

CPSIA information can be obtained
at www.ICGtesting.com
Printed in the USA
FSHW011543190321
79639FS

9 781098 074425